Hilary Glow lectures in arts management and cultural policy at Deakin University. She has also taught Theatre Studies at the Victorian College of the Arts School of Drama, and Australian Studies at the University of Melbourne. In 2007 she was an Honorary Research Fellow at the University of Melbourne's Australian Centre where she also completed her PhD in 2006. Previous to her academic career, she worked for the Australian Film Commission as Manager of the Women's Film Program, and in the Australian theatre sector as an editor and dramaturg. She has been a theatre reviewer and arts commentator across both print and broadcast media.

Photo: Ponch Hawkes: ponch@vicnet.net.au

Bruce Morgan as Kennett Boy in the 1998 Melbourne Workers Theatre production of *Who's Afraid of the Working Class?*. (Photo: Viv Mèhes)

POWER PLAYS

Australian Theatre and the Public Agenda

HILARY GLOW

Currency Press, Sydney

First published in 2007 by
Currency Press Pty Ltd
PO Box 2287
Strawberry Hills NSW 2012 Australia
www.currency.com.au
enquiries@currency.com.au

National Library of Australia Cataloguing-in-Publication Data:
Glow, Hilary.
  Power plays : Australian theatre and the public agenda.
    Bibliography.
    Includes index.
    ISBN 9780868198156 (pbk.).
    1. Dramatists, Australian - History and criticism. 2. Dramatists, Australian - 20th century - History and criticism. 3. Dramatists, Australian - 21st century - History and criticism. 4. Political plays, Australian - History and criticism. 5. Playwriting. 6. Nationalism - Australia. I. Title.
  A 822.3

Publication of this title was assisted by the Commonwealth Government through the Australia Council, its arts funding and advisory body

Australian Government

Australia Council
for the Arts

Cover design by Kate Florance, Currency Press
Typeset in Revival 565 BT 10.5/14.5pt
Printed by Southwood Press, Marrickville, NSW

Contents

Photographs

Acknowledgements

This book began life as a PhD thesis, but the terms of its investigation emerge from my long-standing interest in Australian drama and the people who write it. In particular I have been fascinated by those works which have, over the years, filled Australian theatres and cinemas with bold ideas and a preparedness to challenge the way we see the world. As a dramaturg I have worked with a number of different playwrights over the past twenty years, and this has prompted my interest in the question of what Australian dramatists chose to write about, and why. And this led to the next point of inquiry: what does it take to produce a drama of bold ideas that engages and challenges its audience?

Another key strand of my interest in this field comes from my experience of teaching at the Victorian College of the Arts in the School of Drama from 1982–89. This was an important time for theatre making when students – actors, writers, directors and animateurs – were all encouraged to understand the relationship between theatre-making, people's life experience and the stories they had to tell. Graduates from that era were developing their work in the belief that theatre could (and should) be politically informed and socially inclusive. As a teacher at the VCA I was witness to these developments, which in turn helped to shape both my own dramaturgical practice, and the perspective which guides this book.

I am indebted to the playwrights who agreed to be interviewed for this project and who were so generous with their time and their insights: Andrew Bovell, Patricia Cornelius, Reg Cribb, Ben Ellis, Wesley Enoch, Hannie Rayson, Stephen Sewell and Katherine Thomson. Thanks are also due to the many other writers I spoke to along the way: John Romeril, Susie Dee, Michael Gurr, Timothy Daly, Guy Rundle and

Andrea Lemon. The artistic directors Rosalba Clemente, Robyn Nevin, Simon Phillips, Aubrey Mellor and Tom Gutteridge also made time to talk with me despite busy schedules, and their advice helped me to determine the selection of writers interviewed for this book.

I would like to thank my principal supervisor Kate Darian-Smith and co-supervisor Angela O'Brien who helped bring the PhD to fruition. I am grateful to both of them for their guidance. Thank you to the University of Melbourne for awarding me an honorary Research Fellow position at the Australian Centre, and Deakin University for giving me a sabbatical via an Outside Studies Program Grant which gave me the opportunity to turn the thesis into this book. The University of Melbourne also contributed to the publication through the Publication Grants Scheme and the Faculty of Arts Publication Grants Scheme.

Numerous colleagues have provided help as well as practical assistance: Deakin University librarian Alex Leknius was unfailingly helpful along with Stella Minahan, Anne-Marie Hede and Ruth Rentschler. Clare Wright gave me much sound advice at the start of the journey. I particularly thank my colleague, co-researcher and good friend Katya Johanson for her intelligent and incisive reading of the penultimate draft.

I owe thanks to my family: Lotte, Glenn, Peter, Roslyn, Andrew, Wendy, Daniel, Kate and Ben. I am especially indebted to Lotte and Glenn Mulligan who patiently and attentively read every draft. Their editorial advice, feedback and intellectual engagement in the project was a boon and I am deeply grateful to them. And to my dear friends: Andrea Lemon, Andrea Rieniets, Jane Allen, Amanda Smith, Sophie Inwald, Marea Jablonski and Vivia Hickman who have been encouraging and good humoured over this long process.

Special thanks to Victoria Chance and staff at Currency Press for their encouragement and determination to see the book published.

Most of all, I am grateful to my wonderful and patient family – Bob Burton and my children Josh and Tom – who have put up with the entire lengthy enterprise.

Some of the material in this book has been published in the *International Journal of the Humanities* and by Currency Press.

To Bob, Josh and Tom

And my mother, Lotte

Barry Otto as Max in the 2003 Pork Chop production of *Last Cab to Darwin*. (Photo: Wendy McDougall)

INTRODUCTION

Political theatre

In 2004 the British playwright David Hare, hosted by the Melbourne Theatre Company, delivered the annual John Sumner lecture. His lecture had a bold title, 'Obedience, Struggle and Revolt'. Hare spoke of the particular business of writing political theatre – a task that has defined his entire career, and it was clear that everyone in the audience was paying careful attention. There was, he explained, ginger in the politics of Britain in the 1970s and the UK theatre scene burgeoned. Political theatre was captured by the Left – either by those who championed 'Revolt' or by those who advocated 'Struggle' – a coup decried by the Right which saw theatre turned 'from a place of harmless, corroborative entertainment into a boring dissenters' pulpit'. So, while one side wanted Hare to preach more, the other was keen for him to preach less. But his point was that in this time of political tension, and in the context of dramatically dichotomous political views, theatre seemed 'extraordinarily important … it aroused strong feelings. We argued over it as if it were life itself'. It was a time which Hare looked back upon with 'rheumy-eyed nostalgia'.

For Australian theatre practitioners in the audience there was much with which to identify. Australian theatre also experienced a flourishing of opportunity and talent in the 1970s during a time of pronounced political tension between Left and Right. There are many theatre practitioners today who feel that, by comparison with the 1970s, Australian theatre is languishing with local drama struggling to find sufficient or even adequate production opportunities. Perhaps, too, Hare's account alerted the audience to the critical relationship between vigorous public political debate and a dynamic theatre scene. Theatre seemed important in the 1970s because it addressed issues

1

such as censorship, women's rights, and the anti-war movement, and thereby engaged with a public conversation about socio-political values and beliefs. Does theatre do this now? And furthermore, are there Australian playwrights who take politics, and the ideological debates over Australian values, to be at the heart of their endeavour? These questions are the starting point of this book; and the book is informed by what a group of contemporary playwrights have to say about their purposes and their plays. Talking to these artists made it clear to me that there are, indeed, Australian playwrights who regard the theatre as a forum for political debate, and who want their work to contribute to it.

Eight playwrights were interviewed for this book: Stephen Sewell, Hannie Rayson, Katherine Thomson, Andrew Bovell, Ben Ellis, Reg Cribb, Wesley Enoch and Patricia Cornelius. They are a diverse bunch and as a group they represent established writers (such as Sewell), as well as the newly emergent (such as Ellis). There is a generational spread: Sewell began writing in the 1970s; Bovell, Rayson, Thomson and Cornelius in the 1980s; and Enoch, Ellis and Cribb in the late 1990s. They come from different states: Sewell and Enoch have been based in both Queensland and New South Wales, Cribb and Bovell are from Western Australia (Bovell now lives in South Australia), Rayson, Ellis and Cornelius are from Victoria, and Thomson is from New South Wales.

These playwrights are not like the 'New Wave' artists that emerged out of the Australian Performing Group (APG) in Melbourne and the Nimrod in Sydney in the 1970s – a generation of theatre practitioners whose shared goal was to produce what Julian Meyrick describes as 'pugnaciously nationalistic' theatre (2002:5). The group of writers discussed here do not constitute a 'wave' of like-minded artists; they belong to different generations and their work manifests a range of styles and aesthetic priorities. However, what they have in common is a passion for theatre as a place for public political engagement. And they see their theatre practice as a catalyst for that engagement.

The plays discussed in this book are a diverse group of works but they have in common the task of grappling with the notion of Australian-ness in general, and Australian politics in particular. The

Howard government came into power in 1996 and these plays are meditations on the way it has used that power. They take up the central socio-political debates of our time: race and racism, history and identity, class, power and state control. And they do so in order to engage audiences in a critical public conversation about what it means to be Australian.

Australian theatre has a long history of staging the nation; of plays and productions which have explored Australian themes and highlighted the national politics of the day. And the plays and playwrights discussed here are a part of that tradition. But contemporary political theatre is taking place at a particularly difficult time. Since the mid 1990s Australian cultural policy has taken an economic rationalist approach: tending to favour instrumentalist rationales for culture (measuring the value of culture in terms of its economic and/or social benefits) over the notion of its inherent value (art for art's sake). When Labor Prime Minister Paul Keating released *Creative Nation* in 1994, it ushered in a new era of cultural policy compelling creative producers across all artforms to focus on market expansion through cultural tourism and audience development. In other words, arts organisations were to be exposed to the same market forces as non-arts industries.

The economic rationalist approach to arts policy and funding intensified under the Howard government. It has produced some distinctive benefits for the arts sector: notably the incorporation of a more diverse set of activities (for example multimedia and digital arts) in the 'cultural' category; and it has delivered a new and heightened level of public recognition of what is now referred to as the cultural or creative 'industries'. On the debit side, however, is the necessity for arts organisations, in developing their programs, to place commercial viability above other considerations. For many Australian theatre companies this has meant programming plays which guarantee bums on seats. This means that mainstream companies are increasingly disinclined to stage risky work.

Flagship arts organisations such as the Melbourne Theatre Company (MTC) and the Sydney Theatre Company (STC) have experienced a comparative decline in government funding and an increased dependence on box office and corporate sponsorship. This is not to suggest that the Australia Council is unsupportive of Australian theatre, indeed it has been a major force in determining how the writers discussed here developed their skills and careers. However, the comprehensive take-up of the arts industry model has seen the development of a policy and funding environment in which the small–medium theatre sector has diminished, lessening the opportunities for emerging writers to have their work shown. Leading artists and commentators like Robyn Archer and Rodney Hall have noted that the present policy environment has reduced opportunities for experimentation and failure, and, instead has focused on the bottom line as the key marker of success. Archer notes that: 'currently in Australia the lion's share of arts subsidy is … going to the spectacular … In Australian culture right now, size definitely matters' (2005:40). Archer, Hall and others have noted that the emphasis on an industrial or economic rationale for the arts may well be to the detriment of the creative processes which underpin the sector's long-term viability.

In this environment of reduced opportunity, theatre companies make programming decisions on the basis of box office appeal. This, then, is a critical moment for thinking about the viability of locally made theatre, particularly political theatre which deals with controversial cultural concerns and is probably not the kind of sure-fire box office hit that commercially-minded theatre companies are looking for.

Defining Political Theatre

But here, before we're even out of the starting gate, we have a problem of definition: are not all plays political in the sense that they seek to present a particular point of view as persuasively as possible? Any attempt to identify and define political theatre runs up against this dilemma. It is a function of what Baz Kershaw calls 'the new promiscuity of the political' (1999:16). The idea (originating with the 1970s feminist movement) that the *personal* is political has come to mean that *everything* is political. The mere fact of social existence can be seen as political, so how can the term continue to be used as a meaningful analytical category? In attempting to draw a line in the sand Terry Eagleton writes: 'Keeping goldfish could be political but isn't inherently; like any social practice, it becomes political only when it assumes reference to the processes of legitimating or challenging systems of power' (1980:383). The *raison d'être* of the plays that are the subject of this book is their interrogation of systems of power. While the Indigenous plays celebrate cultural difference they are also profoundly political in how they understand politics as a fundamental, material force in people's lives. Together the plays discussed here seek to understand how politics shapes who we are; it informs how we live and work, our beliefs, values and aspirations.

But this leads to a second important question – if we can assume that political theatre is a meaningful and useful description of a particular set of theatre practices, what then can be said about their political efficacy? Is there an objective measure by which the impact of political theatre can be judged? The answer is no. Kershaw makes the point that an audience's reactions to political theatre are a relative matter: 'it all depends just where you are standing when. A piece of performance may have tremendous political resonance for its audiences, but someone somewhere else is bound to find it ideologically vacuous' (1999:17). This book then, in choosing to discuss some plays and not others, is inevitably making relativist judgements about their political value. In focusing on a particular group of playwrights it does not give an exhaustive account of contemporary political theatre in Australia. But this is not the goal here. Rather, I have selected playwrights who consistently produce works for the stage which exemplify a faith in theatre's capacity to identify and challenge systems of power.

Who, then, is this political theatre for? What does the marriage of theatre and politics produce that makes a significant contribution to the culture? It should be noted that I am not addressing those socially-minded theatre practices which have recently emerged within the community cultural development sector. These are theatre productions, usually developed for specific communities (for example migrants or residents of a housing commission), performed in non-institutional performance spaces, and addressing topical community-based issues. Scott Rankin's youth arts project Big hART, developed through collaboration with community participants and exploring such themes as youth homelessness, is a good example of this kind of work. Such projects are political because they are underpinned by an ethos of participatory democracy, they address contemporary social issues, and seek to empower the communities in and for which they are performed. It is important work.

But this book has another focus – it looks at those plays which have been produced in traditional theatre spaces and watched by (largely) middle-class audiences. This is the site, and the set of practices, conventionally described as 'mainstream' theatre. Perhaps it is an odd place to look for a theatre of social change – after all it is here in this bourgeois precinct where the impact of commercial imperatives is most evident. What does political theatre in this environment seek to do? And why do those writers who are politically motivated choose to write for the theatre when, unlike film or television, audience numbers are so comparatively small? The American writer Alisa Solomon offers insight into these questions when she argues that the theatre is a lifeline 'into the ferocious undertow of our hypermediated culture' (2001:4). Theatre, as a live event, is a challenge to audiences and demands something more of them than, say, watching television in the comfort of one's lounge room. As for the question of why political playwrights might choose to write for the mainstream, Solomon posits the following hypothesis:

> ... because the theatre-going public – college-educated, middle-class – are among the folks who most consistently vote, most frequently write to their congresspeople, and most reliably engage in local civic activities ... More important, plays make ideas palpable ... Other politically minded theatre projects may build or celebrate community, galvanize a protest, involve participants in the collective solution of a predicament. Plays, though, more powerfully than any other form, can ignite dialectical thinking and challenge the moral imagination (2001:4).

The writers interviewed for this book all grapple with the territory outlined by Solomon: in particular, the potential for politically defiant writing in the theatre to challenge its audience. And like Solomon, the writers are concerned with the question of how contemporary theatre can be an effective catalyst for public debate. Playwright Hannie Rayson, for example, sees her role in writing mainstream plays as being one where she: 'engage[s] with the forums of power': 'I do want a theatre which engages and challenges [audiences] in mainstream theatres. I want a theatre which engages with the world they live in. The French radicals actually use the word *engagé* for radical thinking which comes to grips with the world as it is. It's a term which is brimming with energy and optimism. A good mantra for a playwright.' (Rayson 2003a).

Mainstream Theatre

The work of each of the writers discussed in this book embraces a range of styles but they are all 'mainstream' playwrights whose work is performed in and by the leading state-subsidised theatres in Australia. Echoing Pierre Bourdieu's class analysis of cultural tastes, Rachel Fensham and Denise Varney point out that mainstream theatre is defined by the bourgeois audience it serves which, in Australia, is largely comprised of 'an aging Anglo-European middle class ... [sharing] a set of cultural values and identifications marked by similar tastes and patterns of behaviour, language and customs' (2005:46). The mainstream is important because it has national reach. Indeed, the advent of national touring and co-productions by mainstream companies from the early 1990s has delivered greater audience access to Australian theatre. Geoffrey Milne points out that this has helped to 'blur state boundaries, shrink vast distances, and offer audiences all over Australia a greater sense of engagement with, and access to, a national drama' (2004:19). This engagement with national audiences is important for writers who share a concern to put the discussion of national politics on the public agenda for the widest possible audience.

Given that these writers seek opportunities to influence public opinion, as Fensham and Varney have noted, 'the mainstream remains the most powerful frame for the production of public speech' (2005:48). But within this frame there are competing ideological tensions. On the one hand, the writers insist that their highest motivation is to provide politically informed debate on key issues in the public domain. On the other hand the theatre companies that produce their plays are increasingly concerned to program commercially successful work. This makes for a tension between the stated objective of the writers – to produce politically dissenting work with its concern to unsettle the preconceptions of audiences – and the commercial imperatives of mainstream theatre.

One of the palpable outcomes of this tension is the ongoing preponderance of naturalism as the dominant dramatic form. When these writers choose to work within the powerful and potentially influential frame of the mainstream it brings with it a corresponding set of choices to favour the formal elements of naturalism such as a unified narrative, psychologically plausible characters and emotional engagement – all hallmarks of conventional mainstream theatre writing and production. The fact they present their political critique within this mode may account for their having been produced in the first place. Helen Thomson, for example, discussing the mainstream profile of female writers like Joanna Murray-Smith, Hannie Rayson and Katherine Thomson, suggests that the most successful women dramatists are those who 'conform most nearly to the text/character/ narrative paradigm, the "masculine norm"' (1998:114).

The writers interviewed for this book, then, work (with some degree of variation between them) within the conventional and normative modes of naturalistic theatre. Within the framework of mainstream theatre, thus reaching a wide audience, they produce significant contributions to the politicised discussion of key issues in the public domain. Since these writers seek to influence public debate, mainstream stages provide the optimal setting. The widespread media discussion in 2005 of Rayson's play *Two Brothers* when it opened at the Melbourne Theatre Company is a case in point. This politically challenging naturalistic drama, with its provocative account of government asylum seeker policies, caused public outrage. It was the fact of its production at the MTC, with its wide reach and large middle-class subscriber audience that provoked much of the furore. It is no accident that these writers, motivated by the desire to stir up public discussion, choose the mainstream theatre as their platform.

The Interviewees

As we have seen, the group of writers who are the subject of this book cannot simply be identified in terms of their generation: it would be misleading to think of them as the 'Next Wave' following in the wake of the 'New Wave'. But they do share some important characteristics.

In the interviews the writers were asked to make statements about their motivations as playwrights producing work for the contemporary Australian stage. Each discussed their own work and was asked to reflect on its engagement with contemporary public debates. The key and common feature of their self-definition is that they understand their work as explicitly 'political' in the sense that they are engaged in the task of 'challenging systems of power'. Their work is also 'political' in the sense that Jeffrey Goldfarb defines as 'principled critical action' which is not simply a matter of Left–Right politics but a commitment to 'bringing ... discovered truth to the people' (1998:14).

The writers' responses to the question of political theatre – its definition and purposes – can be encapsulated as principled critical action in relation to three overarching frameworks: the moral, the intellectual and the cultural.

Within the 'moral' category are explanations of their motivations and self-definitions which emphasise 'truth telling'. The idea of theatre as a mechanism for making truth claims is resonant for these writers. Stephen Sewell, for example, makes a case for truth telling as part of the process of representing the 'real' – for him is a primary political purpose for art:

> I would say [that] ... people in authority, the last thing they want any artist to do now is to represent the real ... art is a very complex thing – I totally disagree with Brecht when he says food first, morals later. I think morals come first in the way we are constituted. And I think ... people were making art as soon as they were people. Morals come first not in values but in what we are. We make art, we think morally ... The conclusion that I [am] tending towards is [that] the uglier the world becomes, the more diabolically dangerous the world becomes, the more [those in] power want ... artists to divert into things that have nothing to do with what is actually happening to us ... The philosophical issues of truth and the 'real' have been part of our culture for 3000 years, but when it gets to the point of people actually denying that the truth exists, that seems to me not only obscene but characteristic of a culture that is in terrible crisis (Sewell 2003a).

Sewell's insistence on the moral dimension of arts practice leads him to a critique of postmodernism with its relativist reading of truth and morality. By making truth relative, he suggests, postmodernist art becomes an ideal mask for the diversionary tactics of 'people in authority'. Terry Eagleton agrees, arguing that postmodernism's love affair with 'the hybrid and pluralistic' has been much to the advantage of capitalism (2003:119).

If the moral dimension of theatre practice or truth telling is an important characteristic of the way these writers rationalise their practices, then so is the second category – the intellectual dimension. The term 'intellectual' is used here as a means of signifying an emphasis (identified by the writers) on the theatre as a forum for discussion, debate or conversation about ideas. The relationship between intellectual activity and public discussion is a well established one in the literature on the role of the public intellectual. As Goldfarb puts it: 'Free and often contentious public discussion is what intellectual life is all about … A key intellectual role in democracy … is talk. Talk is what Socrates literally did with his life, and stimulating informed talk, public deliberation in an age of information … can contribute to the public good' (1998:35).

All the writers interviewed stated that engaging in debate was one of their highest objectives. Thus Bovell described his primary task as 'generating ideas'; Ellis wants to 'open up discussion'; and Cribb seeks to ask questions so that audiences 'think for themselves'. This highlights one of the persistent themes which emerged from the interviews – the idea of the theatre as a 'public facilitator', as Ellis puts it (Ellis 2005). It derives from the writers' interest in current social and political issues; issues which – as Bovell describes it – 'ask questions about culture and place' (Bovell 2002a). Such descriptions might be thought to be generally applicable to anyone who writes for the theatre. David Hare says: 'It is hard to understand why anyone would choose to go into the theatre in the first place unless they were interested in relating what they make happen on a stage to what is happening off it' (2005:108). Hare suggests that playwrights, almost by definition, are likely to see their work as facilitating public debate. The distinguishing point here, though, is that these playwrights want to facilitate debate by addressing fundamentally political issues exploring questions of power and its taken-for-granted *modus operandi*.

A good example of this is evident in Hannie Rayson's discussion of her play *Life After George* where she notes how the play's production at the MTC in 2000 provoked public debate about the impact of economic rationalism on universities:

> I do know with *Life After George* that it ... created a lot of ruffled feathers; the Vice Chancellor felt he had to write a riposte to it, and there was a lot of stirring-up in the higher echelons of the universities and within the academic community. I think because economic rationalism occurs insidiously, people find it hard to pinpoint, and you don't know who is to blame. And every institution, not just the universities, were going through this experience, so naming those things, to say this is actually happening, is very important. Making clear what all the different lines of argument are – that's an important function for any writer interested in writing towards social justice – that you outline what the debates are. *Life After George* gave ammunition to people who felt unsettled and yet were too busy at work to figure this stuff out, and it showed that they are part of a growing group of disenchanted folk whose shared values, consensual values, and their belief in core values have been completely undermined (Rayson 2003a).

Rayson's account of the effect of her play gives evidence of the potential impact of theatre writing on public debate.

Ellis also sees the importance of theatre as a means of provoking public debate, though he seeks to avoid didacticism: 'I don't want to clamp some kind of message onto the stage and say, come in and do this, look upon my works. I like the idea being a public facilitator ...' (Ellis 2005). Ellis goes on to argue that producing debate is more critical in the current political environment which he sees as having only limited opportunities for the airing of a range of views: 'Our avenues for political discourse have closed down so much so that when we have plays about ... topics that we haven't really discussed a lot, I think audiences want to hear that ...' (Ellis 2005). Rayson's emphasis on stirring up public debate, and Ellis' concern that the theatre remains an effective platform for public discussion, convey some common strands in the thinking of all the writers interviewed for this book. This thinking reflects Goldfarb's view that principled intellectual activity, by definition, stimulates public deliberation.

The third framework within which political theatre is understood by the writers is defined by cultural concerns; in particular, thinking critically about the nation and the nature of identity and belonging. Andrew Bovell outlines the importance of this critical enquiry to his self-definition as a writer for the theatre:

> I want playwrights to be brave and courageous … to be prepared to not be liked; to not be popular if that is what it needs to be. But I want actors, artists to talk critically about our culture – that is what I've continued to do in a lot of my work … I am trying to ask difficult questions about the culture and place I live in … There is no shortage of material that we need to deal with as a culture. As a playwright I would be negligent not to attempt to deal with those large things (Bovell 2002a).

All the writers see the critical framing of the culture as an integral part of their role and self-definition. For example, for Cribb it is the relationship between the city and the country; for Bovell and Enoch it is race and cultural identity; for Cornelius it is class, and for Rayson and Thomson it is an examination of the big ideological shifts in Australia, from social liberalism to neo-conservatism, which provides the basis for the critical cultural analysis offered by their plays. So, while this group of playwrights are interested in a range of different subjects, they share an understanding of political theatre as a matter of principled critical action entailing truth telling, facilitating debate (or deliberation), and examining and testing the conventionalising of cultural beliefs, assumptions and expectations.

The Plays

The discussion of the group of plays that follows takes a particular and distinctive approach. This book is neither an exhaustive history of playwriting over the past ten years, nor is it a work of performance analysis. The performance studies approach is often focused on the task of theorising audience experience and the range of significatory and interpretative possibilities that a performance can embody.

Fensham and Varney point out that the business of watching theatre is 'a complex social act' characterised by the construction and exchange of 'identification and reciprocating desires between the stage and the auditorium' (2005:58). However, the approach to the analysis that follows focuses less on the question of how we watch theatre, and more on the reading and analysis of written (and published) texts. So, my analysis is text- rather than performance-based, and concerns itself with the political contexts and ideological questions which informed the writing of these dramatic texts.

This book also documents how a group of artists have chosen to respond, through their work, to the immediate socio-political environment. This model for analysing the role of the playwright is a move away from some of the traditional readings of the role of the playwright as teacher, propagandist, reformist, or reflector of reality. Instead, these writers are presented here as engaged in a public 'conversation' with their audiences about the important matters of the day. And they do so, as Goldfarb has put it, in the interests of 'cultivating civil society' (1998:203).

The plays are grouped into chapters, each of which explores a particular socio/political issue. While each chapter takes up different themes, the linking idea which informs the analysis is that they critique hegemonic nationalist discourses and dissent from the dominance of neo-liberalist thinking. Not only do these plays deal with explicitly political issues; they also provide an intellectual engagement with unpacking those taken-for-granted ideas which define the times. It is important work for the theatre to be doing and, arguably, attests to the power of the theatre to act as a platform for the independent public discussion of the issues of the day. As Kauffman points out 'it is not easy to describe what is really happening in our culture' (2002:155). This book contends that the Australian theatre of the last decade has been a good place to find out 'what is really happening'.

Chapter 1 looks at recent works for the stage by Indigenous writers. The past decade has seen an increased profile for works written and created by Indigenous artists. This chapter discusses the development of the one-person show as the dominant genre for Indigenous theatre practices, and investigates the relationship between autobiography/

biography and the exploration of both individual and community experiences. The plays discussed in this chapter are different to the others in the sense that they tend to be personal and anecdotal. But they are political in how they represent a shift away from conventional representations of Aboriginality towards a more self-determined expression of political and cultural identity.

Chapter 2 addresses the issue of race and racism through a discussion of dramas which deal with the notion of 'whiteness'. In particular, it focuses on the way in which non-Indigenous writers have grappled with the political issue of reconciliation in the light of the Howard government's stance on Indigenous issues and the vexed question of Australia's history of race relations.

Chapter 3 looks at a group of recent plays which are set outside the major cities. This setting provides an exploration of rural and regional Australia and its diminishing power base, as well as an opportunity to reflect on the nation as a whole. The country town, in these plays, is a metaphor for the nation and facilitates a scrutiny of taken-for-granted notions of identity and belonging. The analysis of this group of plays takes into account a range of related political issues which emerged in Australia in the late 1990s including the effects of economic rationalism, globalisation and the rise of Pauline Hanson's One Nation party.

Chapter 4 deals with issues of class and power as explored in contemporary drama. It discusses how the process of national definition is made more complex and contested by globalisation and industrial change. The plays investigated here document the impact of recent economic changes and the triumph of free-market philosophies on people's lives.

Chapter 5 looks at plays which deal with asylum seekers and refugees, informed by the events of the Tampa crisis in 2001 and the various subsequent incidents related to the arrival and processing of refugees in Australia. This issue, and its treatment in these plays, goes to the heart of current public debates about Australian national identity and values.

The final chapter discusses plays which address the nature of state power. In particular, these are plays which acknowledge the social production of fear in the post-September 11 political environment.

Each of the plays in this chapter address the relationship between state-sanctioned security measures, the rationale for increased state power and the discourses of democratic freedom.

Critical Nationalism

The cultural economist David Throsby has identified key federal government policy issues and suggests that they be understood in terms of their cultural implications (2006). These issues – economic policy, immigration, Indigenous affairs and Australia's independence – are all central to the plays discussed here. They offer a critical reading of the economic, social and political terrain, and in so doing they question those cultural values which inform current hegemonic definitions of nation and nationhood.

While providing a critique of the nation, these writers also conjure with it; using familiar iconography, idioms and characters they seek to create a world, and to tell stories, which are readily identifiable as 'Australian' by Australian audiences. The ambivalent or critical nationalism which these plays evince has echoes of Ghassan Hage's notion of 'affective attachment' within society. Hage sees two kinds of 'affective attachment' to the nation; one that is 'caring' and the other 'worrying'. The caring society is one that 'generates hope' and induces citizens to care for it; whereas the culture of worrying 'such as the one we have in Australia today' produces a defensive society and forms of 'paranoid nationalism' (2003:3). The plays here act as a critique of 'paranoid' or defensive nationalism while at the same time manifesting a 'caring' attachment to the images of nation they produce.

In producing a body of work for public consumption that is informed by critical nationalism, these playwrights are operating within the domain of the public intellectual, using the theatre as their platform. Said argues that successful intervention in the public sphere, one of the hallmarks of public intellectual activity, requires a platform which is relatively unencumbered by powerful interests, that is, 'by the very antagonists one resists or attacks' (2002:29). Using a theatrical metaphor taken from Jonathan Swift, Said looks to the 'stages itinerant' to provide the solution; stages are 'platforms that either aren't available to or are shunned by the television personality, expert, or political candidate' (2002:29). Said does not include the theatre on his list – the 'stages itinerant' he has in mind are, for example, lectures, pamphlets, radio and alternative journals – but the trope of the stage is particularly evocative here.

Although Australian mainstream theatre has seen a marked increase in the level of commercial involvement and a greater dependence on earnings through sponsorship and box office, it is nevertheless relatively free from the machinations of big business. This 'relative' independence can be measured in comparison with the Australian print and broadcast media with its increasingly concentrated ownership. It is, perhaps, not surprising then that writers find the theatre an appropriate setting not only for the staging of their work, but for their contribution to the discussion of key issues on the public agenda.

Theatre as Countervailing Voice

In offering a thematic reading of ideas of place, race, history, class and power, this book shows how closely these plays are related to their political environment. In general terms, they can be read as a repudiation of the Howard government's rhetoric around one nation. Indeed, they present a series of pictures of the nation as fundamentally divided. These plays see generational, racial and class-based divisions as being primary and defining characteristics of the nation. In a political environment dominated by hegemonic nationalist discourses of 'one people, one nation', they are an important countervailing voice.

Voicing a countervailing view is a vital cultural activity. After all, one might ask, what are the consequences of *not* doing so? If art merely produces 'positive' images of the world, then we are left with all the limitations of a mono-culture. Kauffman writes that the moral majority in the USA seeks to police the conceptual parameters of art in order to preserve family values – and this has the potential to produce cultural product which 'is the equivalent of the kind of movies you see on airplanes: nothing too controversial, too sexy, or too disturbing. Airplane movies and airplane art – like Norman Rockwell's – feed us images we already have of ourselves. They never make us uncomfortable, or challenge our most cherished conceptions' (2002:156). In this way, Australian theatre (when it's good) is something of an antidote to the valorisation of the ideals of 'relaxed and comfortable' – national ideals famously touted by John Howard.

But the plays discussed here are not simply oppositional. They add to the mix of views that are emerging in the public domain about our national identity and values. They bespeak a liberal humanist perspective: the young protagonist Felix in Rayson's *Inheritance*, Bea in Thomson's *Navigating*, Max in Cribb's *Last Cab to Darwin*, and the lively voices that can be heard in contemporary Indigenous theatre – all reflect a sense of optimism about both the capacity for truth seeking, and the possibilities for social and political engagement in contemporary Australian life. That our mainstream theatre is a site for such dialectical thinking is significant. While we may no longer feel, like David Hare and his contemporaries did in the 1960s, that theatre is as important as life itself, we might however see Australian theatre as challenging ideological conformism and engaged in an urgent political task – to speak against the grain of the neo-liberalist enterprise.

Deborah Mailman in the 1995 Kooemba Jdarra production of *The 7 Stages of Grieving*. (Photo: Tracey Schramm)

CHAPTER 1

INDIGENOUS IDENTITIES

Aboriginality is remade over and over again in a process
of dialogue, imagination, representation and interpretation
Marcia **Langton** (1993:33).

Over the past decade Australian theatre has seen an increased mainstream profile for works written and created by Indigenous artists. This work is characterised by the dominance of autobiographic and biographic modes of story-telling, and is often presented in the form of the one-person show. This theatre work, in telling intensely personal stories, is markedly different to the political theatre discussed elsewhere in this book. It mostly does not, for example, refer directly to external political events, and even when it does so, the effect is to reinforce a sense of personal and/or community identity. In other words, it is less a drama around political or national 'conversations', and more one about cultural identities. Yet there is no doubt that this Indigenous theatre clearly expresses the political concerns of Aboriginal theatre artists for whom self-determination and self-representation are priorities. Indeed this work is notable and distinctive for capturing the nature of Indigenous experiences within an Australian political context in order to achieve a new set of negotiated meanings between non-Indigenous and Indigenous Australians.

Indigenous writer and director Wesley Enoch sees an explicitly political goal for Indigenous theatre. This was manifest in the first wave of Indigenous theatre writing in the 1970s and 1980s which Enoch describes as having a 'revolutionary' message; plays like Kevin Gilbert's *The Cherry Pickers* and Robert Merritt's *The Cake Man* had a 'strong political fist in the air [and] a didactic message to give' (Enoch

2005). Contemporary Indigenous theatre, however, is marked by a tendency to explore personal stories focused, as Enoch describes it, on education and celebration. Celebratory theatre, he says, is concerned with 'celebrating survival and it's a kind of uplifting thing' (Enoch 2005). The goal to use theatre to educate stems from 'the idea of passing on experiences and passing on knowledge of a community by writing our history on stage' (Enoch 2005).

Non-Indigenous screenwriters and playwrights have long held a fascination for telling the stories of Indigenous peoples. In particular films and plays set in the colonial past, written, directed and produced by non-Indigenous artists, have frequently focused on the suffering meted out to Aborigines at the hands of white colonial masters. *Rabbit-Proof Fence* (2002) was based on the book by Indigenous writer Doris Pilkington Garimara and adapted for the screen by non-Indigenous filmmakers Christine Olsen and Phillip Noyce. Its unsettling portrayal of Aboriginal children being forcibly taken from their families under the *Aboriginal Protection Act* in the 1930s, was seen by many as a powerful critique of Australia's race-based assimilationist policies and occasioned 'an outpouring of sadness ... by non-Indigenous viewers' (Potter 2004). In the theatre, too, non-Indigenous playwrights have frequently tackled Indigenous stories and themes.

While these post-colonial critiques by non-Indigenous screenwriters and playwrights contribute to ongoing debates about race and the history of racism, there remains a significant concern about Indigenous self-representation and self-determination. Indigenous academic and cultural theorist Marcia Langton points out that the signifying practices of non-Indigenous cultural producers are critical because they inform the broad Australian understanding of 'Aboriginality' such that: 'The most dense relationship is not between actual people, but between white Australians and the symbols created by their predecessors. Australians do not know and relate to Aboriginal people. They relate to stories told by former colonists' (Langton 1993:33).

Recent work by Indigenous theatre writers represents a shift away from the familiar strategies and figures of conventional discourses of Aboriginality, towards a political theatre in which self-representation is the key rationale and purpose. This is a culturally significant activity in a political environment which has seen the derailing of the reconciliation project. Michael Dodson, Indigenous activist and human rights campaigner, argues that while the Howard government's focus on practical measures for addressing Indigenous disadvantage has been important, so is the key symbolic gesture of an apology and the acceptance of responsibility for the many 'unresolved issues' between Indigenous peoples and the state (Dodson 2004). In the absence of such an acknowledgement, Dodson argues, there has been a failure 'to understand that recognising past injustices helps to transform the trauma of victimisation into a process of mourning and allow for rebuilding. Respect is owed to those who have suffered, and this may play a part in their healing and that of the nation' (2004:136).

The political role of Indigenous theatre, then, is two-fold: firstly it engages Indigenous audiences in a process of cultural recognition, education and celebration. Secondly, it engages non-Indigenous audiences in an intercultural experience where past and present injustices are recognised and respect is paid to Indigenous peoples and their communities. In the process, 'whiteness' is destabilised as the default position. White audiences come to understand the way race defines the lived experiences of Indigenous Australians. And while government policy emphasises practical reconciliation, Indigenous theatre engages audiences in a symbolic process of 'healing'. In Indigenous theatre the question of cultural identity is politicised and shown to be shaped by race and racial difference. For white audiences, at least, there is an understanding of the plurality of Australian-ness.

Background to Australian Indigenous Theatre

In her historical account, Maryrose Casey (2004) points out that Indigenous theatre started to gain a profile and greater access to Australian main-stages from the 1960s. The civil rights movement in Australia, which had seen an outpouring of public political protest in that decade, also prompted the development of a range of new Australian theatre work, in particular the APG and the Nimrod Theatre. This activity, both political and theatrical, was a catalyst for a commitment to develop and fund Australian arts, including Indigenous artists who were funded through the Australia Council's Aboriginal

Arts Board. Since the 1970s a number of Indigenous theatre artists – notably performers, writers and directors – have emerged. A seminal figure was West Australian Indigenous playwright Jack Davis who, in partnership with white director Andrew Ross, produced a series of groundbreaking works for the Black Swan Theatre Company from the late 1970s to mid 1980s. Davis' writing for the theatre, which included the plays *Kullark* (1979), *The Dreamers* (1982) and *No Sugar* (1985), was celebrated for representing the resilience of Indigenous communities in the face of the assimilation policies of successive Australian governments. The Broome-based musical *Bran Nue Dae* (1990), written by Jimmy Chi, was another significant production which achieved unprecedented success during its nationwide tour in 1993–94. Katharine Brisbane sees the success of this production, its broad appeal and joyous celebration of Indigenous experience, as a 'turning point in the … history of Aboriginal writing for the theatre' (Brisbane 1995).

In the 1990s three Indigenous theatre companies emerged: Ilbijerri Theatre in Victoria (1990), Kooemba Jdarra in Queensland (1993), and Yirra Yaakin in Western Australia (1993). Their work has emphasised the diversity of Aboriginal experiences, languages and cultural practices, helping to dispel the notion of a single, homogenous Indigenous voice. The development and production of Indigenous theatre throughout the 1990s should be seen in the context of the reconciliation movement. In the first half of the decade, the Keating government raised the profile of Indigenous issues in the broader community and, after the High Court's 1992 *Mabo* decision, tackled the question of Indigenous land rights claims. For Keating, the *Mabo* decision was a critical moment in the debates around nationhood because it provided an opportunity for white Australians to recognise Aboriginal culture as a defining element of Australian identity. In this political environment Aboriginal theatre came to greater prominence helping to deliver a broader recognition of Indigenous culture and achievements.

The increasing importance of recent Indigenous theatre can also be understood in terms of its growing profile within mainstream theatres where it is seen by mainstream audiences. Among a number of catalysts for this move is the success of Bangarra Dance Theatre which has attracted international attention for Indigenous performance arts. A growing number of Indigenous theatre artists who have graduated from professional theatre training courses offered by flagship institutions such as the Victorian College of the Arts in Melbourne, the National Institute of Dramatic Arts in Sydney, Queensland University of Technology in Brisbane, and the Western Australian Academy of Performing Arts in Perth have also made an impact. And there have been specific opportunities for some Indigenous writers and directors to develop and showcase their work. The Indigenous Branch of the Australian Film Commission, for example, has provided project and professional development opportunities for Indigenous writer/ directors, including theatre-based practitioners, to develop their screenwriting and directing skills and to produce short film projects.

In 2002, in a collaboration between Ilbijerri Theatre and Playbox, six new Indigenous works were produced for a mainstream audience. The season, entitled *Blak Inside*, provided a professional theatre experience for more than forty Indigenous actors, writers, directors, designers and trainees; and it also achieved a new level of profile for this work which had previously experienced 'a long history of struggle for stage space' (Mellor 2002:iii). A decade ago, Katharine Brisbane argued that the growing national recognition of Indigenous theatre was a function of the fact that Indigenous artists are 'at the forefront of our arts ... Today Aboriginal drama is ... the most important new Australian voice and one which will, in due course be the most widely heard in other countries' (Brisbane 1995). The current level of international touring for Indigenous arts, across all artforms, suggests that Brisbane was prescient on this issue.

Biography and Autobiography

A consistent feature of much contemporary Indigenous theatre writing is its emphasis on biography and especially autobiography. This focus on subjective narratives based on lived experience bears out Hage's point that Indigenous people do not see themselves as part of conventional Australian history. Indigenous people, he argues:

> ... do not relate to and cannot appropriate 'Australian history' ...
> because what is posited as Australian history is simply not history

> from their perspective. In this sense they have their own history
> – or, more exactly, their own pool of histories ... to appropriate
> memory from (Hage 2003:91).

This emphasis on 'their own pool of histories' is manifested in the choice of autobiography/biography as characteristic modes of storytelling for Indigenous writers. Watson shows that a characteristic feature of the autobiographies of Indigenous writers is how they 'employ the rhetorical power of witnessing' which means that these writings testify from personal observation 'to present their accounts of history through their bodies ... so that the telling of their stories is, literally, an embodiment of history' (2002:13). Moreton-Robinson maintains that: 'self-representation by Indigenous women is a political act'. It is political because these are self-representations which emphasise the practical, political or personal attributes of a life lived in a society which constructs Indigenous women as 'other' (2002:3).

There are numerous examples of autobiographic theatre work by Indigenous theatre-makers, among them, *Page 8* (2004) by David Page and Louis Nowra, *White Baptist Abba Fan* (1997) by Deborah Cheetham, *Thumbul* (1996) and *Lift 'Em Up Socks* (2000) by Tom E. Lewis, *Gulpilil* (2004) by David Gulpilil and Reg Cribb and *Little Black Bastard* (2004) by Noel Tovey. Arguably a prototype for much of this autobiographical storytelling in the form of the one-person show is Ningali Lawford's work, *Ningali* (1994). Lawford wrote and performed this one-woman show directed by Angela Chaplin for Deckchair Theatre in Western Australia. It is a highly personal account of her life experiences, from her childhood in the Kimberleys to her adult self-discovery through dance and performance. Its distinctive qualities include direct audience address, the use of several languages, the telling of an intimate and personal story which combines moments of humour with moments of pain and loss. These qualities have come to mark the genre of staged Aboriginal autobiography and, as Helen Thomson has described it, together make for a performance practice which embodies a powerful '"talking back", a decolonising act' (Thomson 2001:25).

Box the Pony (1997) by Scott Rankin and Leah Purcell is another in the genre of the autobiographical one-woman show. The story is an intensely personal one with Purcell playing herself, her mother and grandmother, as well as a plethora of other characters as she revisits the pub, schoolroom, the meat packing plant and the Murgon beauty pageant of her past. This work mediates stories of racism and violence with moments of irreverent humour. Casey observes that the combination of strong emotion and humour characteristic in these works is a method by which the work offers a 'fearless engage[ment] with contentious and fraught issues that exist under the surface both between indigenous and non-indigenous people, and within indigenous communities' (2004:201). As in *Ningali, Box the Pony* emphasises the role of women in Indigenous communities. We see that the three generations of women in Purcell's family have produced a powerful bond, and a kind of resilience that has seen Purcell survive and triumph in her career as a writer/performer. Hage notes that the relation of Indigenous people to injustice is one characterised by 'endurance and resistance' (2003:95) and this is borne out by much of the work which underlines the cultural significance of endurance.

Tammy Anderson's *I Don't Wanna Play House* (2002) and Richard Frankland's *Conversations with the Dead* (2002) were two of the six plays in the season of new Indigenous works, Blak Inside, produced by Ilbijerri Theatre and Playbox Theatre in Melbourne in 2002. Anderson's one-woman show is a journey through childhood told in a candid, unsentimental way with Anderson playing all the roles including her mother, father and grandmother. As in *Box the Pony*, this story is intimate and autobiographical as Anderson tells of her mother's systematic abuse at the hands of a series of violent boyfriends. There is redemption, though, in the story's celebration of survival against the odds, the strength of the mother–daughter bond, and the sense of belonging that this engenders. Again the theme here is one of endurance, and also of witnessing. Anderson as a young girl is a witness to her mother's suffering and we as the audience are, in turn, led into the role of witness. There is no hiding from the ugly truths of this testimony. This is also a rhetorical feature of Indigenous women's autobiographical fiction where the revelation of the unpleasantness of aspects of lived experience is a repeated trope. As a rhetorical strategy it 'makes manifest those hidden and hurtful events of history' and its function is to provoke a response from the reader – 'the uglier the truth, the more emotional impact' (Watson 2002:9). Anderson's play evidences a similar approach with its uncompromising portrayal of contemporary Indigenous life and the economic, racial and gender constraints that impact on Aboriginal women as they go about their daily lives.

Frankland's play *Conversations with the Dead* (2002) is based on his experience as a field investigator for the Royal Commission into Black Deaths in Custody in the late 1980s. After its first season in the *Blak Inside* program, the play was subsequently re-mounted in a new production directed by Wesley Enoch for a successful season at Sydney's Belvoir St Theatre. The play's protagonist, Jack, tries to come to grips with the terrible sense of loss experienced by grieving relatives of the dead. In the process of documenting these tragic preventable deaths, Jack struggles with the emotional cost to himself. This autobiographic account is structured around a series of horrifying episodes of racism, injustice and despair. The play also reflects Frankland's background as a musician and poet incorporating songs, music and poetry. Frankland's play is for 5 actors (and one musician) and is therefore formally different to the one-person shows discussed above. But it shares with them some distinctive characteristics: in particular the emphasis on public grieving, the symbiosis of the experiences of the individual with those of the community, and the role of the audience as a witness to suffering. Like the other plays, too, it is focused on the notion of healing; the idea that storytelling and singing, and the recounting of moments of anguish provoked by injustice, is a step towards spiritual healing.

Stolen

Alongside these autobiographical works are biographical ones. *Stolen* (1998), an exploration of the experiences of the 'stolen generation' written by Jane Harrison, was commissioned by Melbourne's Ilbijerri. The play was written in response to the 1997 report, *Bringing Them Home*, by the Human Rights and Equal Opportunity Commission which detailed the history of forced assimilation of Indigenous families into white society. Harrison based her writing on the testimonies and anecdotes of Aboriginal people who had been taken away as children from their families. The play tells the stories of five Aboriginal people and traces their lives as they grow up in institutions or with white families; often frightened, abused and suffering the terrible grief of enforced separation from family and community.

Directed by Wesley Enoch in a co-production between Ilbijerri and Playbox Theatre, *Stolen* was hailed by both audiences and critics and the production toured extensively around Australia, followed by seasons in London, Hong Kong and Belfast, and a further re-mounting in Australia in 2002. The play was significant not only because it spoke to current issues around reconciliation, but it insisted that the suffering of Indigenous people be acknowledged as a contemporary reality. At the end of the play, the actors step forward on the stage and, using direct audience address, speak of their own backgrounds and experiences. This device has two immediate outcomes; first, the facts of the stolen generation become not simply a matter of history but a present-day concern. Second, the diversity of the actors' own stories demonstrates that there is no one Aboriginal story, no overarching Aboriginal view or voice, but a multiplicity of experiences and cultural practices. In this way, the play integrates the personal with the political; it interconnects biography with autobiography, the individual with the community, and the historical with the contemporary. The interlocking of these elements, and the importance given to witnessing history through lived experience, is a signal feature of much contemporary Indigenous theatre and it makes a distinctive contribution to contemporary political theatre in Australia.

Yanagai! Yanagai!

A more recent work, also based on community research, is *Yanagai! Yanagai!* (2003) written by Andrea James. First produced by the Playbox Theatre in a co-production with the Melbourne Workers Theatre, the play subsequently toured Yorta Yorta country and had seasons in England and Wales. The play is a direct response to the loss of a native title claim by the Yorta Yorta people in 2002. According to the ruling of the High Court of Australia the traditional connection of the Yorta Yorta people to the Murray River and surrounding land had been washed away by 'tide of history' (James 2003:i). James wrote her play with the participation of Yorta Yorta artists, in response to this decision. The play, she says, is a 'right of reply'; an opportunity to repudiate the Court's judgment by showcasing vibrant traditional and contemporary cultural practices.

The play interweaves three storylines. The first story is a mythical account of the spirit Munarra, and her two dingo companions. The Munarra story is from the dreamtime and tells us how the Dhungula (Murray) river was created. The second story tells of the colonial appropriation of the land and river by Sir Edmund Curr, one of the first white men to move in to the territory (the words 'Yanagai! Yanagai!' mean 'Go away' and were the first recorded Yorta Yorta words spoken to the invading colonists). The third story is set in the present and focuses on the character of Uncle Albert who is persuaded to attend the High Court hearing in order to testify about the destruction of a sacred site, only to find that his testimony is discredited and ultimately ignored. This portrait emerged out of James' observations of the experiences of Yorta Yorta elders as they took to the witness stands during the title claim proceedings: '[they] came back ... ashen and shaken by days ... of relentless and calculated questioning designed to break down, dismiss and counter Yorta Yorta culture in a hostile and culturally insensitive environment' (James 2003:ii). Using the reminiscences of these people, James has constructed a picture of their lives, and the play becomes a portrait of their political struggle for land rights and cultural recognition.

Yanagai! Yanagai! and *Stolen*, like the other Indigenous theatre work discussed here, also reflect on the nature of personal and collective memory. These works are often a celebration of survival, and an assertion of how 'otherness' and states of marginality can be seen as sources of energy and potential change. These works represent a move towards self-determination and an attempt to wrest back control of the images and stories that are produced about Indigenous people and their experiences. Indigenous artists in both film and theatre are grappling with representation and self-representation. As Tom O'Regan has argued, Indigenous people:

> ... object to stories that they do not create, or at least, co-create

because such stories impact on them. These stories provide the wider community with ways of 'knowing Aborigines' which Aborigines then need to negotiate. The imbalances involved in this 'authoring', see the Aboriginal emerge as a 'figure of discourse' (1996:277).

The 7 Stages of Grieving

Wesley Enoch is an Indigenous theatre artist who has made a significant contribution to contemporary Indigenous theatre both as a writer and director. In addition to co-authoring *The 7 Stages of Grieving* (1996) with actor Deborah Mailman, Enoch has written *The Sunshine Club* (1999), *Black Medea* (2000) and *The Story of the Miracles at Cookie's Table* (2007). As a director, he has directed Jane Harrison's *Stolen* in 1998, Richard Frankland's *Conversations with the Dead* in 2002 and Tony Briggs' *The Sapphires* in 2004.

Like *Stolen*, *The 7 Stages of Grieving* reached a broad audience; a national tour in 1996 was followed by a fully re-mounted touring production in 2002. It is a contemporary personal story of an Aboriginal woman reflecting on her family, her culture and traditions, in order to provide what Gilbert calls a 'panoramic view of Aboriginal life' (1998b:92). This work is of particular interest because, like *Stolen*, its setting of a personal story within a specific political and historical context struck a chord with Australian theatre audiences at a time when the issue of reconciliation was high on the public agenda. It is a personal story and not strictly autobiographical, but so prevalent is the autobiographic form within Indigenous theatre that the play retains elements of the form. Another more recent example of this blurring of autobiographic and biographic storytelling is David Milroy's *Windmill Baby* (2005).

Indeed, Enoch sees his play as a 'constructed autobiography' where the story of the protagonist has a metonymic relationship to the stories of others in the Indigenous community (Enoch 2005). In discussing his approach to the making of work, Enoch outlines his understanding of the materials of storytelling through collaborative theatre-making:

> There is a sense of gathering, about participation and ... respecting everyone's input along the way. And listening with your heart. That sense of thinking: that rings true, that's got a

> real kind of integrity, that story has a bigger metaphoric meaning
> than just your life, your story, it's got something else that rings
> true … you can say that's more of a universal story, or if we put
> it on stage it's more than just one person's story, and [it] can
> resonate for a whole community (Enoch 2005).

As Watson notes this 'invoking' of the community's stories is also a familiar device in contemporary Indigenous fiction. It implies that while a particular story of individual experience is being told, 'others in the community could tell similar tales' (2002:14).

The 7 Stages of Grieving sees the phases of Aboriginal history as a movement from the dreamtime through invasion and genocide to assimilation and then to self-determination and, finally, to reconciliation. It tells this sweeping history through a personal narrative of an Aboriginal woman as she negotiates her life in the present while grieving for the past and the suffering it has inflicted on Aboriginal people. The story of this Aboriginal woman (and the stories she narrates for the audience) simultaneously embodies both an individual narrative and the larger contextual history of Indigenous oppression and injustice. This parallel storytelling that places the individual's story within the context of the community's story is often reflected in the detail of the dialogue:

> I am in a crowd. I'm in a crowd of people walking. I'm in a
> crowd of people all walking along in silence. I'm in a crowd all
> walking along in silence, my Dad, my brothers and sisters and
> my Nana. No one speaks, no one yells, everyone just walking
> together (Enoch & Mailman 1996:60).

This account of an Indigenous protest march has the individual's point of view wrapped up in the group's experience, while the rhythm and repetition of the speech gives power and momentum to the anecdote. Enoch privileges the role of storytelling in his theatre practice, indeed for him the work's political impact is tied up with its storytelling; he says that the play 'has a very strong political element to it because it is a telling of stories, an empowering of those stories with a political edge to it. But it's still primarily about story-telling, about people' (Bradley 2000:65).

Short scenes or fragments made up of poems, songs, chants, dances and stories are meditations around the theme of grieving. This grieving for the familial and cultural loss incurred through past injustices is a rich vein running through the work. The narrator tells us:

> Sometimes I let myself go and find myself crying in the dark alone, without my family and home. The pain comes in here, I cry and cry until I can't feel anymore ... Then I wake up ... and I have got my home ... and I have got my family ... and I will never have to live through what my Dad has been through (Enoch & Mailman 1996:48).

The themes of weeping, remembrance and the proximity of the past for current generations are powerfully present in this work. As in *Ningali*, there is also an emphasis on the value of family and community ties which are a cause for pride and celebration. Enoch comments that the play reflects the view that 'You may not have land, or language, or culture [but] I do have my family and I have my home and I do have a place that I call my own ... often the discourse is about what's been taken from us. How do we shift that to ... what is the cultural capital that we have, as opposed to what is missing in our lives?' (Enoch 2005).

Finally, at the end of this grieving for past losses and present injustices, there is a moment in which reconciliation is seen paradoxically as a matter for both questioning and cautious optimism. The word 'reconciliation' is broken down into 'Wreck, Con, Silly, Nation' and the narrator says 'What's the use in having a word if we don't think and talk about it?' (Enoch & Mailman 1996:70). Elizabeth Schafer argues that Enoch and Mailman here have 'ridiculed the entire concept' of reconciliation (2003:63). Indeed, Enoch says that reconciliation is 'a white man's issue'; something that 'white Australia has to deal with' and he acknowledges the important role of non-Indigenous playwrights such as Rayson, Thomson and Bovell in continuing to keep the discussion of reconciliation on the 'white man's' political agenda (Enoch 2005). However, the third and most recent edition of the play (published in 2002) includes a new final scene entitled 'Walking Across Bridges'. This new scene acknowledges the potential for reconciliation and refers to the People's Walk for Reconciliation in May 2000 in which an estimated 150,000 to 250,000 people walked across the Sydney Harbour Bridge in a symbolic gesture of reconciliation.

The play's narrator describes the spirit of hope this public ceremony engendered for many people around the country, 'like a song it caught on ... walking across bridges. Who would have thought, eh? I guess we can't go back now' (2002:73).

Both *The 7 Stages of Grieving* and *Box the Pony* incorporate untranslated traditional language which immediately establishes a culturally specific framework through which the works must be viewed and understood. It privileges the connection with those in the audience who understand the language and puts white audiences in the uncharacteristic position of being the outsiders. As a theatrical technique it calls to attention the relationship between language and power and underlines the reality, vibrancy and currency of contemporary Indigenous cultural life. This is a significant means of challenging the stereotype of Indigenous societies as traditional and unchanging; rather it suggests that the culture's capacity to adjust to new challenges and situations is an important part of Indigenous struggle for recognition and self-determination. Thus, the cultural forms which are represented in these works (songs, dances, stories, traditional language as well as a hybrid English patois) are not merely relics or atavistic remnants of traditional cultural practices, but very much part of the lively, diverse and contemporary experience of Indigenous Australians. Gilbert suggests that in these works tradition 'functions ... as an inheritance through which contemporary Aboriginality can be negotiated' (1998b:76).

Enoch seeks to produce theatre, primarily, for Indigenous audiences. He says:

> If we think that our audiences are really just a non-Indigenous audience then it's not exciting any more. Whereas ... the audience I want to play to is an audience that already has a lot of understanding of Indigenous issues be they white or black doesn't matter, you don't have to keep playing the teacher to them. And spoon feed them along all the steps of the way, if you can just ... jump into this part of the debate, that's where we can create some really interesting stuff. I'd much rather do that (Enoch 2005).

The objective is explicitly political – 'I want to create social change by telling stories. I want it to be an active decision on the behalf of the audience that they change an aspect of their prejudices or their actions and that they can go into the world and change it somehow by looking at these plays and these stories' (Enoch 2005). Enoch does not seek to produce a polemic – instead, he argues, audiences also need a 'human experience' when they go to the theatre. The theatre needs to give them 'not just an intellectual armoury but also an emotional, experiential armoury to go into the world and tackle issues' (Enoch 2005). Enoch gives the example of *Stolen*:

> Yes, you can read about it in the newspaper and … you can read about the stolen generation, but then if you come to see a play there is a reference point for an emotional response that people can talk from and that's a very human thing and a humanising thing so that these political messages and these dry facts and figures actually have a human component … (Enoch 2005).

Enoch's political objective for his work is realised by building up a more complex set of images, histories and meanings around 'Indigenous' people than has existed to date. He seeks to 'build a picture which is not homogenous; there is not just one frame of seeing things … It's the cumulative sense of what being Aboriginal is in this world which is so much more interesting' (Enoch 2005). This greater diversity of images and stories furthers debate within Australian society about Indigenous issues and rights.

For Enoch the political objectives of his theatre work, and the work of other Indigenous writers, is to build cultural continuity. As each generation dies, so too do the oral traditions of much Indigenous cultural practice and belief and, thus, Enoch argues contemporary Indigenous theatre needs to 'connect us with where we come from and [give us] choices about how to construct our own identity as Indigenous people' (Enoch 2005). The purpose of this theatre practice is to address the question of:

> … how to make yourself stronger to face things in an individual or community way. It's not about how we deal with [the white community], it's how do we deal with ourselves … I think Indigenous people have perpetuated our own misery … If you actually go, I am empowered, I am strong, I know where I come from and I know who I am, I can deal with everyone as an equal. I can look you in the eye … that kind of confidence to me is really important (Enoch 2005).

An Intercultural Exchange

The work of these Indigenous theatre-makers demands an acknowledgement and revaluing of Indigenous experience. It challenges conventional representations of Indigenous people as part of 'nature', or absent from history as implied in some canonical Australian accounts. Some of the work is concerned to acknowledge power relations and to recognise the role of language in making what is social and constructed seem transparent, real and 'natural'. In doing so it explores the dichotomy of black/white while at the same time playing with the notion of essential difference/sameness. Perhaps the most signal characteristic of this work is that it shows how 'otherness', states of marginality, or plurality can be seen as sources of energy and potential change.

While the work emphasises the commonality of experience, it is also distinctive for its steadfast insistence on the individual nature of the personal story. Moreton-Robinson explains the paradox in this way:

> All indigenous women share the common experience of being indigenous women in a society that deprecates them. Accordingly, there will be common characteristic themes dominant in an indigenous woman's standpoint ... Such a standpoint does not deny the diversity of indigenous women's experience. Indigenous women will have different concrete experiences that shape their relations to core themes (Moreton-Robinson 2002:75).

The emphasis on autobiography and personal stories in Indigenous theatre acts as a means of destabilising and contesting an all-encompassing, fixed Indigenous identity. This underlines what one critic describes as an 'explanation of Aboriginality as a process of continual becoming' (Gilbert 1998b:77). While the Indigenous community is often seen by white Australia as a single and undifferentiated entity, it is in fact, as Langton has argued, made up of a great diversity and plurality of voices and experiences, and thus 'there is no one kind of Aboriginal person or community' (1993:11). There is an assumption, says Langton, 'that all Aborigines are alike and equally understand each other, without regard to cultural variation, history, gender, sexual preference and so on' – it is a belief, in other words, that 'there is a "right" way to be Aboriginal' (1993:27). Indigenous theatre artists are creating work to destabilise such beliefs and common sense ideas which could be seen as the product of white Australia's fear of difference. The Indigenous writers discussed here do not assume they can speak for others, or on behalf of anyone else. In this sense, their work represents a repudiation and deconstruction of essentialism, and the universalising totality of the undifferentiated 'other'.

An Australian National Opinion Poll (ANOP) study conducted in 1985 ('Land Rights Winning Middle Australia') describes the 'predominant stereotype' of Australian Aborigines held by 'middle Australians'. The stereotype is of a 'primitive, nomadic people who are passive and lazy, and have become virtual alcoholics under the influence of white society' (quoted in Goot & Rowse 2007:170). Such a stereotype, and indeed the very notion of 'middle Australians' is contested by Murray Goot and Tim Rowse who argue that even if there was such an entity as 'middle Australians', then their thinking on this issue 'would not be unitary'. However, while they are right to query the terms used by ANOP, this stereotype of Indigenous people has been repeatedly reinforced and re-affirmed through media representations of contemporary Aboriginal life. Such a view of Indigenous people might also account for the popular support by 'middle Australians' of John Howard who has disassociated himself from land rights issues and the reconciliation process.

An alternative perspective on this issue comes from Guy Rundle who argues that the 'cultural community' in Australia is attracted to certain features of the aboriginal community. The 'cultural community', he says, is drawn to the notion of a kinship culture in which 'mutual obligation, reciprocity and at-homeness in the wilderness were constitutive of individual subjectivity and meaning' (Rundle 2007). Aboriginal culture provides an alternative to 'the standard dilemmas of the postmodern inner city – a sense of isolation, attenuation, a lack of shared meaning and groundedness, of a sense of the real'. Rundle's notion of a 'cultural community' can, of course, be problematised in the same way as ANOP's notion of 'middle Australians'; he is relying on a stereotype of the liberal, cosmopolitan inner-city Australian.

But his point helps to fill out the picture: the 'middle' Australian conception of Indigenous people as lazy, nomadic and primitive sits at counterpoint to the attraction of Indigenous culture felt by inner city liberal Australians. Both sets of ideas are, inevitably, generalised and mythologised and mask the specific complexities of Aboriginal life and politics.

One of the achievements of the plays discussed here is in their intercultural exchange. The idea of 'Aboriginality' is re-negotiated and re-made by deconstructing conventional, mythologised and iconic representations. Rather than perpetuating a white gaze apprehending Aboriginal people as 'object', these Indigenous artists are producing work in which they are the subject; they are performing themselves, engaging both Indigenous and non-Indigenous audiences, and holding out hope for genuine reconciliation as the result. This is explicitly political theatre – theatre which takes a critical stance into the public domain. Watson points out that Indigenous autobiographic accounts pull the audience into a relational act of witnessing and this involves the 'necessary transference of political awareness' from performer to audience (Watson 2002:29). This relational exchange is specifically political as Indigenous autobiographies are written: 'to educate, to initiate change, to witness history through personal lived experience' (2002:38).

The works discussed here produce theatre which reflects on the past and explores the nature of personal and collective memory. Above all else they are a celebration of survival, and an assertion of the ways in which 'otherness' and marginality can be seen as sources of liveliness, creativity and potency. This highly personal theatre is, unavoidably, also highly political; it is taking place within a context where the process of reconciliation has stalled while the Australian federal government refuses to acknowledge and address the many 'unresolved issues' between Indigenous peoples and the state (Dodson 2004:135).

This work asserts the values of diversity which is an antidote to the hegemonic rhetoric of one nation. It works to alert audiences to the experiences and stories of contemporary Indigenous peoples which, while inarguably 'Australian', sit outside conventional readings of national identity. These writers, therefore, are fulfilling Gilbert's injunction for the Australian theatre of the new millennium to play a key ideological role: to 'dilute the cultural power of whiteness by embracing heterogeneity and difference' (Gilbert 2003:26). This is a call for a politically engaged theatre practice – a practice which impacts on the national public discussion and is in evidence in contemporary Indigenous theatre.

Scott Johnson as Tom and Pauline Whyman as Edie in the 2003 HotHouse
Theatre production of *Wonderlands*. (Photo: Jules Boag)

CHAPTER 2

THE HISTORY WARS

This 'black armband' view of our past reflects a belief that
most Australian history since 1788 has been little more than a
disgraceful story of imperialism, exploitation, racism, sexism
and other forms of discrimination. I take a different view. I
believe that the balance sheet of our history is one of heroic
achievement and that we have achieved much more as a nation
of which we can be proud than of which we should be ashamed
John Howard (1996).

The issue of race and racism is at the heart of much contemporary
cultural debate about national identity and history. While Indigenous
themes, stories and characters, written by both Indigenous and non-
Indigenous writers, have appeared in many Australian plays and films
since the 1970s, in the present political climate the task of addressing
white–black relations in Australia has a new ideological force. The
dominant view of the past, with its emphasis on the 'heroic achievement'
of European settlers, is countered in the plays under consideration in
this chapter. Here the focus is on the representation of race and, in
particular, the relationship between racial politics and national history
as exemplified in plays by non-Indigenous writers Andrew Bovell and
Katherine Thomson. The plays critique the hegemonic nationalist
discourse (exemplified by the opening quotation) and produce
alternative versions of the nation and its identity.

The Political Context: Land Rights and Reconciliation
In the mid-1990s, and with the election of the Howard government
in 1996, Australia found itself in the midst of what Ghassan Hage
(2003) has called a 'memory war'. This struggle over national memory,

and the consequent debates around national responsibility, came to the fore as a result of a number of key events. The *Mabo* decision had been handed down by the High Court of Australia in 1992, with the court deciding in favour of Indigenous claims to be the rightful owners of land that had been under state control in Queensland and northeast Australia (High Court of Australia 1992). Indigenous land rights were further enshrined in the *Wik* Decision in 1996 when, in a second landmark case, the High Court handed down a decision that the granting of pastoral leases did not automatically extinguish native title (National Native Title Tribunal 1996).

In the following year, 1997, the Human Rights and Equal Opportunity Commission released the report, *Bringing them Home: Report of the National Inquiry into the Separation of Aboriginal and Torres Strait Islander Children from Their Families* (Human Rights and Equal Opportunity Commission 1997). The report details the systematic and forced separation of Indigenous children from their families, putting them into the foster care of white families and state institutions, with a view to forcing the assimilation of 'half caste' children into white society. The play *Stolen*, discussed in the previous chapter, is an account of what happened to some of the children who had been separated from their families and who became known as the 'stolen generation'. In May 1997, in commemoration of the passing of the 1967 referendum on Commonwealth powers over Aboriginal affairs, a Reconciliation Convention was held (Australian Reconciliation Convention 1997). It had been expected that at this convention Prime Minister Howard would take the opportunity to apologise to the Indigenous community in an official acknowledgement of the responsibility of Australians, and their colonising predecessors, for the harms done to the colonised; but instead Howard delivered a personal apology which was viewed and 'widely condemned as cold and mean-spirited' (Brett 2003:198).

Howard's continued refusal to support a formal apology for past injustices is based on the belief that such an apology would implicate present generations in accusations that should only apply to their predecessors. This belief was informed by Howard's critique of the 'black armband' view of history that he felt had dominated during the

Keating years. For Howard, this was as a negative view of history which meant that:

> even people's confidence in their nation's past came under attack as the professional purveyors of guilt attacked Australia's heritage and people were told they should apologise for pride in their culture, traditions, institutions and history and should feel guilty for wrongs committed generations ago. Too often displays of guilt over actions which today's Australians would never condone, for which they are not guilty and should not be made to feel guilty were substituted for practical proposals to right the consequences of past wrongs (Liberal–National Party 1988:7).

This was the genesis of Howard's commitment to the idea of 'practical' rather than symbolic, reconciliation. Thus, it became evident as the reconciliation movement gathered apace in the late 1990s, that instead of an apology the Howard government would insist that its policy focus be on the causes of disadvantage in many Indigenous communities in the areas of health, education, housing and employment.

Settler/Invader Plays

Over the past decade a body of theatre work, written by both Indigenous and non-Indigenous writers, has responded to the debates on reconciliation, land rights and the stolen generations. This body of work is in a sense the most recent wave of postcolonial theatre writing concerned to identify and deconstruct the forms and tropes of colonialism. Earlier exemplars of post-colonial theatre writing emerged in response to Australia's Bicentenary in 1988. Gilbert argues that this period was marked by the writing and production of what she calls 'settler/invader plays' which attempted to 'come to terms with the histories of dislocation, convictism, and oppression of Aborigines' (Gilbert 1998a:98). Playwrights such as Michael Gow, Stephen Sewell, Louis Nowra and Janis Balodis provided illustrations of 'the broad concerns of a non-Indigenous theatre attempting to find stage images for a past/present that reflects the ambivalence of the settler subject' (1998a:99).

The 'settler/invader' plays, identified by Gilbert, which provided such a trenchant critique of the cultural assumptions behind the

Bicentenary, are not the only Australian plays with Indigenous content. There are also earlier examples of plays by non-Indigenous writers including Katharine Susannah Prichard's *Brumby Innes* written in 1927; George Landen Dann's *Fountains Beyond* (1942), a realist drama set in an Aboriginal settlement on the fringe of a township; Jim Crawford's *Rocket Range* (1947) which looked at the effects of weapon testing on Aborigines; and Oriel Gray's *Burst of Summer* (1960) suggested in part by the experience of Ngarla Kunoth who played the title role in *Jedda*. And from the mid-1970s there emerged a plethora of both films and plays written by non-Indigenous writers looking at Indigenous issues, stories and characters. Possibly the most significant of these in Australian cinema is *The Chant of Jimmie Blacksmith* (1978), directed by Fred Schepisi and based on the novel by Thomas Keneally – a film which, while not a popular success at the time of its release, was an important factor in building the international success and reputation of Australian cinema (O'Regan 1996:59). Films like this, along with *Manganinnie* (1980), and *We of the Never Never* (1982) were part of a re-envisioning of colonial history by non-Indigenous filmmakers. The same cultural and political project can be seen to have informed the work of many non-Indigenous playwrights in the 1970s including: Jack Hibberd's *Captain Midnight VC* (1973), Bill Reed's *Truganinni* (1970) and Dorothy Hewett's *The Man from Mukinupin* (1979). These plays were characterised by their condemnation of white Australia's mistreatment of Indigenous people. This strand of writing continued in the 1980s with such plays as Keneally's *Bullie's House* (1981), John Romeril's *Bastardy* (1982), Tony Strachan's *State of Shock* (1986) and Ray Mooney's *Black Rabbit* (1988). These plays and films understand Australia's colonial past as defined by the oppression of Indigenous people. Further, this body of work shares the view that reconciliation with Indigenous people is a vital public political project.

While reconciliation remains a key objective for the non-Indigenous Australian playwrights considered here, they are operating in a different mode. In plays such as the colonial drama *Black Rabbit* (1988), the violent and overt racism of the white protagonists, Archie and Stanley, is rationalised by their nineteenth-century views of racial difference and white superiority. The Indigenous characters in the play are hapless victims; the two white characters are brutal sadists, and together they paint a picture of racism as a cultural phenomenon of the past carried out by people who did not know any better. A critique of this mode of representation is outlined by the African–American novelist Toni Morrison who points out that: 'the pattern of thinking about racialism [is] in terms of its consequences on the victim ... of always defining it asymmetrically from the perspective of its impact on the object of racist policy and attitudes' (Morrison 1993:11).

Bovell and Thomson attempt to move beyond this 'pattern of thinking' identified by Morrison by interrogating the nature of whiteness itself. In this sense, they are providing something new not only to the public political project of reconciliation, but also to a critical reading of hegemonic nationalist discourses which insist on using history as a means to build a sense of national pride in Australian achievement.

Whiteness

Over the past decade or so, postcolonial critiques around race and racism have been critically informed by the discourses of 'whiteness'. Whiteness is the body of knowledge, ideologies, norms and particular practices that have been constructed in the writing of colonial histories and which affects how we think about race and how we understand our own racial identities. Whiteness is a taken-for-granted social construction and powerful in the way it naturalises the equation between 'white' and 'civilisation' and 'culture'. In his book *White Nation*, Hage tells us that whiteness is a means of positioning the white nationalist as the legitimate manager and controller of the cultural form the nation should take, and that while nationalist discourse is 'not necessarily about excluding or destroying otherness ... [it] is about regulating the modality of its inclusion' (1998:174).

In his subsequent book, *Against Paranoid Nationalism*, Hage goes on to look at the historical construction of whiteness as a racial category. Here he describes what he calls the 'quintessential colonial racist logic': 'Question: Why are Europeans civilised and superior? Answer: Because they are white' (2003:50). Within this 'logic', whiteness becomes the ultimate indicator of 'civilised humanity'. In the plays written by non-Indigenous writers which are discussed in this chapter, the apparent logic and assumptions of whiteness stemming from the colonial period are investigated. In particular, in *Holy Day* Bovell highlights the ideological assumptions of whiteness, and looks at the ways it intersected with class, and evolved in response to the social, economic, and political circumstances of the colonial period.

The plays discussed here address both the historical and contemporary relationships between the white and Indigenous communities in Australia. They scrutinise the reflexive and powerful forms with which whiteness manifests itself in Australian society. In *Holy Day*, in particular, whiteness is seen to be shaped and maintained by class and religion. In describing her impetus to write *Wonderlands*, Katherine Thomson says:

> we are privileged to work with Aboriginal people ... you realise how that enriches the country, or rather my attitude to my country. I don't think I ever want to hear [again] the phrase 'the Aboriginal problem', because Aboriginal people say it's a white problem ... (Thomson 2005a).

Both Thomson and Bovell begin their processes of enquiry with a critical look at the methods by which whiteness excludes the 'other', or regulates (to use Hage's term) the nature of the relationship between Indigenous and non-Indigenous Australians. This investigation of whiteness is a central mechanism for the larger project of constructing a critical and destabilising approach to hegemonic notions of Australian identity and nation. Howard's endorsement of the foundation myth of heroic enterprise and achievement by the white settlers of Australia, and his repudiation of the black armband view of history can be read as a key ideological feature of hegemonic nationalism. These plays by non-Indigenous writers constitute a critique of these dominant forms and mythologies of nationhood. More particularly, they articulate a growing sense of moral failure as the discourse of one nation masks the reality of a divided nation which cannot acknowledge a shared past in which atrocities were visited on one side by the other.

Hage points out that Australia has two antagonistic histories of its colonial past: the history of the colonisers and the history of the colonised (2003:95). It is in the interests of the dominant group, the colonisers, to produce a version of events which make the dominated forget the nature of the conflict. As a consequence, Hage argues, 'to speak of an Australian memory is not politically innocent. It is part of a hegemonic disposition on the part of the coloniser to complete the integration of the colonised into the reality of the coloniser' (2003:94). The plays discussed in this chapter engage with this question of the hegemonic discourses of conventional colonial history. They find ways of politicising memory in order that diverse and alternative histories can be acknowledged. They represent a rejection of the implicit claims of colonial histories that there is only one way to read and interpret the past, and seek to show the limitations of this outlook. Well-known standard histories of colonial Australia, like those written by Manning Clark and Russel Ward for example, ignored Indigenous history entirely, while the more recent historical work of Keith Windschuttle has set out to downplay the brutality and racism of white settlers against Indigenous populations. Windschuttle argues: 'When it is closely examined, much of the evidence for the claims about massacres, terrorism, and genocide turns out to be highly suspect. Most of it is very poorly founded, other parts are seriously mistaken, and a good deal of it is outright fabrication' (Windschuttle 2001).

In addressing the unprecedented emergence of public debate on issues of nation, history and identity, David Carter cites the rise of the historian as a key figure amongst the public intellectuals of our time. Carter says: 'History, especially when it involves what [historian Inge] Clendinnen calls "national morality", is what has made the public intellectual *public*' (Carter 2004:36). This is the background to the public dispute, aired by the Australian media, and known as the 'History Wars', in which Windschuttle has disputed the work of other historians, such as Henry Reynolds. His particular focus has been to contest the calculations of the death toll in the Indigenous population as a result of colonisation. This 'grisly dispute' over numbers, as Stuart Macintyre points out, is only a narrow way of looking at the issue, which might more broadly be seen as a moral argument that is taking place on the national stage; like Clendinnen, Macintyre sees that 'the mediation between past and present is a profoundly moral activity' (2004:5).

This attempt to use history as way of grappling with 'national morality' is a shared feature of the plays discussed here. In both *Holy*

Day and *Wonderlands*, there is an explicit concern with the writing of history and this provides an opportunity to explore how institutional and cultural forces, reflecting the knowledge, ideology, norms, and practices of whiteness, not only contributed to a system in which white people profited over Indigenous people, but which established the taken-for-granted paradigm of whiteness against which, by default, everything else continues to be measured.

Holy Day

Andrew Bovell's play *Holy Day* constructs a complex portrait of colonisation. It is a description made thick through the juxtaposition of multiple dichotomies: black/white, male/female, old/young, English/Irish, innocence/experience, faith/atheism, coloniser/colonised. These dualities which turn around issues of gender, race and class intersect throughout the play to create a sense of an historical moment defined by a complex network of power relations. Thus the victimiser, the coloniser, is also him/herself the subject of oppression and can be understood as a product of the era's ideological frameworks. But Bovell's play is not simply concerned with accurate historical details – it also speaks metaphorically to audiences about the very recent past and, indeed, the present.

The play uses the signs and symbols of colonisation, in particular the classic iconography of the lost child. Peter Pierce has argued that the 'abiding force' of the figure of the lost child comes from its symbolic representation of 'the anxieties of European settlers' and stands for 'the apprehensions of adults about having sought to settle in a place where they might never be at peace' (Pierce 1999:xii). Bovell takes up this territory and further interrogates its symbolic force by asking the question: is a lost black child worth less than a lost white child? The rhetorical power of this question is palpable as it underlines the assumptions which have rationalised white Australia's policies towards Aboriginal people, in particular the forced removal of Aboriginal children from their families.

The play has had two major productions across three mainstream theatre companies: the first production, directed by Rosalba Clemente, took place in 2001 at State Theatre Company of South Australia and was followed by a season of the same production at Melbourne's Playbox Theatre. A second production, directed by Ariette Taylor, was part of the STC's 2003 season. Set in the mid-nineteenth century, the play centres around the Traveller's Rest—a halfway house between distant settlements. The first production of the work was designed and directed to emphasise the sense of a vast and barren terrain encircling a small hut representing white settlement. In the opening scene of Clemente's production a huge wooden cross placed at the back of the stage dominated the space; a representation of the attempt by colonisers to assert their dominance, both real and symbolic, over the land and its original inhabitants. Made up of five short acts, the play's central plot concerns a missing white child and, in counterpoint a number of sub-plots are developed which hang around the stories of other missing or stolen children. The play's structure helps to build the metaphoric potency of this work as it uses the trope of the missing child to address broader issues of the history of race relations.

The Traveller's Rest is run by Nora Ryan, a hard-bitten and ruthlessly practical woman who has been toughened by the experience of living by her own wits in a harsh terrain. She inhabits a world dominated by men who are used to having their demands met by subservient women folk. Nora's sole companion is an Aboriginal girl, Obedience, whom she regards as her adopted daughter: 'Her skin might be black but I've brought her up white ... I found her out among the saltbush, abandoned by the mother. Left for the dingoes. She's been with me ever since. She'll look after me when I'm too old to do it myself' (2001:16). This is a complex relationship: on the one hand Nora protects Obedience from being raped and offers her own body to be used instead by the men who visit the Traveller's Rest looking for sex. However, Nora's protection of Obedience effectively enslaves her; she must be obedient and grateful for the paternalistic hand that feeds and clothes her. Obedience is locked into subservience for life. This relationship provides an exploration of the way paternalism appears to justify the ideological premises and discourses of racial difference to itself; Nora thinks of herself as the girl's mother and protector while simultaneously seeing her as an indentured servant with no rights of her own.

Obedience is not the only stolen child in this play. Elizabeth is the missionary's wife who arrives at the Traveller's Rest in a state of distress at the loss of her newborn baby. The baby girl has disappeared and Elizabeth blames the local Aborigines who, according to her account, have never shown sufficient respect, let alone piety, for the missionary zeal of her husband who is also missing in mysterious circumstances. Also arriving at the Traveller's Rest are two men, Goundry and Epstein, along with an adolescent boy, Cornelius. Goundry and Epstein are itinerant white workers, ex-convicts leading a hand-to-mouth existence, moving around the country seeking labouring or farming work. As the narrative unfolds it becomes clear that Goundry has forcibly taken Cornelius from his home and routinely sexually abuses the boy. And to guarantee Cornelius' silence, Goundry has cut out the boy's tongue. The catalyst of the play's action is the missing baby; Elizabeth's unproven accusations set off a chain of events culminating in the massacre of the local Aboriginal community by a group of white settlers, all too readily stirred up by Goundry, and keen to take the law into their own hands. The pious Elizabeth is told to take comfort from the fact that the blacks take good care of their children:

> WAKEFIELD: ... if they have her she will be safe.
>
> ELIZABETH: It is not their children we are talking about. But a white child ... If we lose her to the desert then she is as good as dead, for she is condemned to wander aimless and Godless ...
> (2001:27)

The idea that her child has been taken by 'the blacks' into the wilderness is, for Elizabeth, an irredeemable descent into entropy. And it is this which makes the lost white child an evocative metaphor for the fear, and desire for mastery, which defines much of the history of the white invasion and colonisation of Australia. But the systematic and shocking enslavement of children (both black and white) by the white colonisers is, in Bovell's vision, an unacknowledged horror in Australia's past establishing legacies of secrecy and abuse for future generations to negotiate.

Bovell discusses the importance of the grimness of the play and its lack of redemptive qualities:

> In exploring white history and racism in a contemporary form

the choice was to make it unrelenting, unpalatable, to make it
as grim as I possibly could. Aubrey Mellor [Artistic Director
of Playbox Theatre in Melbourne] argued passionately and
furiously about its bleak ending. He made a couple of points to
me that were really interesting in terms of this whole debate …
I didn't deal with hope, and there is tremendous hope. So in
taking those two young people, the young aboriginal girl and the
young white boy, to such a place of damage I was saying there is
no hope for the future … The other issue for me was the extent
of the damage on the national psyche. The kind of damage that
was brought here by white people, and to make that kind of
damage palatable, to present some hope at the end, would have
been a cop out for me (Bovell 2002a).

The catalyst for Bovell's politicisation as a writer was his experience
in the 1980s of writing for the Melbourne Workers Theatre. Here
his plays dealt with the experiences of working-class life. This
background, he notes, adds to his sense that playwrights need to be
'brave and courageous' and to 'be prepared … not [to] be liked, to not
be popular' (Bovell 2002a). Writing courageously and in an 'unpopular'
vein manifests itself in Bovell's refusal to include any redemptive
moments in this play's portrait of Australian race relations. It produces
an uncompromising view of race and racism in Australia – and allows
Bovell to portray the legacies of the past and their impact on attitudes
and responsibilities in the present. Further, in this portrait Bovell has
deconstructed some of the deep ideological premises of whiteness and
its implicit assumption of 'civilisation'. He uses the disappearance of
the white child to tease out the deeply embedded values of whiteness.
The white characters find the notion of a lost white child an almost
unthinkable moral transgression; a transgression of the 'natural' order.
The unreflexive and unexamined assumptions that shape 'whiteness'
are highlighted for audiences who see that an assumed racial superiority
equates white society with 'civilisation', and that this assumption is the
premise for the entire colonial enterprise.

The play develops a critique of paternalism in order to deconstruct
the rationale which led to the forcible removal of Aboriginal children
from their families. Both Nora and Goundry are self-appointed
guardians of children who are not their own, and both exploit their

charges. But Nora sees herself and her actions as well-intentioned rather than self-interested. In her terms, Nora has not stolen Obedience, but 'rescued' her; she has not enslaved the girl, rather she has housed, fed and protected her. Nora's paternalism is rationalised by her sense of her good intentions. This exposure of the politics of well meaning paternalism is a theme that is also taken up in Hannie Rayson's play *Inheritance* (discussed in Chapter 3). In both cases, the writers portray a deeply embedded pattern of racist thinking by whites which continues in the present day. Bovell paints a picture of nineteenth century colonial attitudes to race and racial difference, and uses it as a parable for contemporary audiences. Indeed, the paternalism which was used to justify the generations of stolen children is well within the living memory of many of the play's audiences, bringing the contemporary relevance of this historical play into sharp relief.

The white characters in *Holy Day* inhabit a matrix of complex and often contradictory positions defined by their socio-economic status and their gender. Thus, for example, Nora's dominance over Obedience is understood and played out in the context of her own position at the bottom of the social ladder as an unmarried and childless woman running a disreputable establishment. In this patriarchal universe Nora's survival is dependent on playing a subservient role by accommodating the sexual needs of the men around her; she has no piety, no social graces and no ambition to climb the social ladder. She wears her Irish heritage and her anti-English sentiment on her sleeve:

> EPSTEIN: Do you think in England they could ever imagine a sky like this?
>
> NORA: I don't think they give a shit what the sky is like down here. They've sent us to the end of the world, that's all they know. And it doesn't matter what kind of place we make of it. To them it will always be the end of the world. England's sewer (2001:29).

Nora is the familiar figure of conventional Australian cultural stereotypes: she is anti-authoritarian, fiercely independent and anti-British. She despises pretension and values hard work. But this is not the sentimental or celebratory portrait of the spirit of heroic achievement which dominates colonial histories. Instead, Nora is seen as a product of her times, struggling to survive (un-heroically) by taking advantage

Pamela Rabe as Nora in the 2003 Sydney Theatre Company production of *Holy Day*. (Photo: Tracey Schramm)

of those lower than her in the pecking order. Thus Bovell offers a reading of race and race relations in the colonial past which is critically informed by other factors – particularly gender and class – which mediate the play's take on black/white relations in Australia. In this way, Bovell moves away from the reductionist view that racism is the outcome of explicit acts of racism, and instead sees it as the systemic product of a struggle for power and dominance often by people who are themselves disempowered.

Another important feature of the play is its critical re-reading of masculinity and mateship. Mateship in particular is a familiar cultural trope that has been associated with the discourses of the Australian national type evoking ideas of selflessness, a fair go and egalitarianism. The play's critique of the hegemonic discourse of nationalism is notable in its savage deconstruction of mateship. The three men Goundry, Epstein and Cornelius, ostensibly mates and travelling companions, are in fact caught up in a cycle of humiliation, sexual and physical abuse, menace and bullying. Goundry routinely rapes the boy and while Epstein has not participated, neither has he tried to stop it for fear of reprisals from Goundry. The play suggests that this is more than just brutal behaviour in a hard, lawless world. It is the systematic use of power to ensure domination. Thus, Bovell does not provide a conventionalised, sentimental or redemptive portrait of the lives of white colonists giving each other a 'fair go' and facing adversity together, but portrays a society riven by class, gender and racial difference. In such a world a massacre of one group by another – the explosive outcome of a dynamic combination of white power and fear – seems utterly plausible.

While *Holy Day* gives an unredemptive reading of mateship and the ethos of egalitarianism in Australia, it has some features which recall more conventional renderings of Australian colonialism. In particular, the play evokes the Australian landscape in a series of familiar tropes as an unknowable place, inimical to white society and full of threat and foreboding. The white settlers, though in actuality landlocked, feel themselves to be marooned, living 'on a white island in a black sea' (2001:30). These familiar representations of the landscape are recognisable from many Australian films, especially those dealing with white/black relations: in particular, the notion of the bush as inimical to white society (*The Chant of Jimmie Blacksmith* 1978, *Walkabout* 1971); the bush as essentially mysterious and unknowable (*The Last Wave* 1977, *Picnic at Hanging Rock* 1975, *Jedda* 1955); the bush as a place of death and decay (*Blackfellas* 1993).

These familiar tropes have seen the landscape developed as a 'character' within Australian cinema which, as Tom O'Regan has argued, emphasises 'the uncanny and the other-worldly, the mundane and the spiritual, and the tragic clash of Aboriginal and non-Aboriginal peoples in the Australian continent' (1996:58). In a similar way, Bovell has set up a recognisable context for the struggle between the black and white communities in his representation of the landscape which plays strongly on the ideas of 'in place' and 'out of place'. So while the white colonists are engaged in a constant battle to assert their territorial rights, the landscape that surrounds them tells a different story. They are clearly 'out of place'. Whatever sense of belonging they manage to establish for themselves is not only fragile but comes at a terrible cost.

While this view of the landscape and the attempt to give it a distinctive 'character' is also a familiar rhetorical device in Australian historical narratives, Bovell takes a less usual approach in his portrait of the Aboriginal woman Linda. Linda, who has been seen hanging around the Traveller's Rest, is accused of stealing Elizabeth's baby. Without any evidence, the white men shackle her to a post and she is denied food and water until she confesses. The character of Linda is articulate and knowing; she speaks English and has clearly been well acculturated in the ways of white society, while remaining outside it. There is no attempt to provide deep insight into the character and motivations of Linda; Bovell does not speak on behalf of Indigenous people under colonialism.

> [Aubrey Mellor] argued that Linda the Aboriginal woman, who was blamed for the abduction of the child, should have been a more Indigenous woman. By that I think he means she should not have had contact with white people. For me that was the line [which] the white writer can't cross, or you shouldn't cross. I don't think it is our place, or our right, to represent a pre-

colonial aboriginality. That is the business of black writers in this country. So it was very clear to me politically why I had to make that choice, why I had to make her a woman who had had to contend with white men and that she was a product of that in some way (Bovell 2002a).

Bovell sees that as a white writer his job cannot entail representing 'pre-colonial aboriginality'. And he makes the further point that the play does not focus on Linda's point of view as a victim of racism. This contrasts with two recent Australian films, made by non-Indigenous filmmakers, *The Tracker* (2002) and *Rabbit-Proof Fence* (2002). Both are set in the past, and portray the experiences of Indigenous people as they confront a racist white society. The nature of that confrontation is told from the point of view of the victim. Marcia Langton has described this 'genre' of Australian film as emerging from a desire by 'non-Aboriginal people [wanting] to make personal rehabilitative statements about the Aboriginal 'problem' and to consume and reconsume the 'primitive' (Langton 1993:10). Bovell has steered away from this conventional representation by refusing to portray Linda as the 'primitive', and by seeing 'whiteness', rather than Aboriginality, as the 'problem'. His target is the experience of white colonists and he examines the ways in which 'whiteness' has provided a framework by means of which all white/black relations have been historically mediated.

Holy Day looks at the role of history and the historical record in determining our attitudes and beliefs. The struggle over history and its social meanings is manifested in the so-called 'history wars' and the debate over the nature and extent of the damage done to Indigenous communities at the hands of white colonisers. Bovell has understood the ideological role of history in this debate over two competing versions of Australia's past: the triumphalist 'white blindfold' view articulated by Howard in his 1996 Robert Menzies Memorial Lecture (see the quotation at the head of this chapter), versus the so-called 'black armband' view of historians like Henry Reynolds which sees the process of settlement as a violent invasion in which land was seized, and people and entire communities were destroyed (Reynolds 1981). Bovell explores the question of how history itself gets written: by whom, and about whom. The pastoralist, Mr. Wakefield, is keeping a journal because 'a man likes to think that one day his descendants will want to know what life out here was like'. Epstein, the itinerant ex-convict replies: 'I wish I could write. I'd like to think that those that come after us will know about the likes of me, as well' (2001:11). It is a reminder that history is often a one-sided account of the past offered by those who have access to the means of recording it. Bovell is acknowledging here that history is both partial and blind to its own partiality. Further, Bovell wants to analyse the connection between the past and our contemporary understandings of who we are and what we believe. Towards the play's end, Epstein comes to Wakefield to beg his assistance in stopping the massacre, the baying for blood, which Goundry has fomented by stirring up the rumour of the white child stolen by blacks. But Wakefield advises Epstein:

> WAKEFIELD: Turn your eyes away from the river, for once it's done not a word of it will be spoken. It will be as though it never happened.
>
> EPSTEIN: This has nothing to do with the lost child. This is about land and the right to graze your sheep.
>
> WAKEFIELD: We're building a nation here. It can't be done without cost.
>
> EPSTEIN: And what kind of nation will it be?
>
> WAKEFIELD: A proud nation one day (2001:62).

This scene encapsulates many of the play's central concerns: Wakefield advises a strategy of silence and repression as a way of dealing with uncomfortable and inconvenient truths. Wakefield tears out the pages of the journal in which he has been keeping a record of events – a literal manifestation of the suppressive powers of history. Further, Wakefield has the pragmatic view that the expunging of impediments to colonisation is the inevitable product of progress and this, he signals, is the premise upon which nations are built. This valorisation of the twin virtues of progress and pragmatism lies at the heart of triumphalist readings of Australian history. Epstein, on the other hand, reminds audiences that pride in national achievement is spurious if terrible injustices are perpetuated in its name. At the end of this scene a further telling exchange takes place as Elizabeth, looking for sanctuary, comes to see Wakefield:

ELIZABETH: Mr. Wakefield, will you take me … ? I have nowhere else
to go. I am ready to tell you the truth.

He holds up his hand to hold her words back.

WAKEFIELD: Don't … for if you do then I can only turn you away.
But if you stay quiet then yes, I can take you, for a man out here
needs a woman by his side. But this is our agreement, Mrs Wilkes.
You and I will be silent about what has passed. For what is not
spoken will eventually fade (2001:63).

Thus, Wakefield not only finds that keeping silent about the truth is
a historical necessity, but also that repression will effectively mask
suffering. Bovell addresses the power of whiteness to withhold and
suppress historical knowledge, and sees Wakefield's utterance – that
'what is not spoken will eventually fade' – as emblematic of the system
of beliefs that has damaged what Bovell calls 'the national psyche'
(Bovell 2002a).

The play was well received by critics who noted its uncompromising
portrait of Australia's 'history of occupation and oppression' (Hallett
2003). Another review described the play's 'unsparing fictional portrait'
of colonial life: 'a difficult play about difficult history' (Bramwell
2001). The emphasis is on the play's representation of the past and
the reviewers noted the relevance of this historical exploration in
the context of contemporary political debates about national history.
Reviews also warned that audiences were likely to find the play
challenging: one reviewer describes the play as 'tough and demanding'
(Hallett 2003); while another notes that the play's 'relentless and
gripping account of events from first contact' has cultural and political
significance in an environment where 'recent national political debate'
has 'systematically repudiated and belittled' such versions of history
(Bramwell 2001).

This commentary testifies to the play's critical engagement with key
issues on the public agenda. It bears out Bovell's intellectual objective
to grapple with the subject of racism in a way which does not provide
audiences with a redemptive get-out clause. In an interview to publicise
the play's opening in Melbourne, Bovell illustrates the importance of
the relationship between past and present when he comments that the
play is 'a cautionary tale … it's about what's to come rather than what

has just happened' (Vaughan 2001:67). For Bovell, then, his play is not simply about setting straight the historical record, but is a mechanism for thinking about race and racial relations in the present and in the future.

The Chair

After the success of *Who's Afraid of the Working Class* in 1998 (discussed in Chapter 4), Bovell again teamed up with the writers Patricia Cornelius, Melissa Reeves and Christos Tsiolkas, together with composer Irene Vela, and director Julian Meyrick to produce the work *Fever* for the Melbourne Workers Theatre in 2002. Bovell's contribution was the short play *The Chair* (2002b) – and in many respects it continues and intensifies the thematic explorations established in *Holy Day*. In an interview, Bovell describes this short play as 'unresolved theatrically, but I know that I am standing on a precarious edge in that piece. To stand on that edge is quite exhilarating and totally occupying ... I am engaged with seeking meaning – it has not been written from a place of knowing, it's been written in the process of questioning' (Bovell 2002a). The questioning position Bovell ascribes to himself is one which also allows a number of unresolved issues to be flagged for the audience. In particular, this bleak portrait of white/black relations, begs the question about the possibility of achieving mutual understanding between Indigenous and non-Indigenous Australians.

Once again, the work is set in the nineteenth century and explores aspects of colonialism and race relations. A white woman is living alone in a rough cottage and has found an injured Aboriginal man on her property. She takes him inside and tends to his broken ankle, but she is terrified of him, and while he is unconscious, she ties him to a chair and holds him captive. The play opens with the man regaining consciousness and finding himself in pain and bound by ropes. The woman explains:

> I heard you scream. The night here is full of screams. The fox caught in the trap. It sounds like a child. But the hen taken by the fox ... it's like a woman being taken against her will ... And then yours ... What was I meant to do? I should have let you scream ... It's what I usually do. Wait for it to bleed to death ... I could have left you there ... I should have (Bovell 2002b:4).

This scenario sets up a tension between gendered and racial dynamics. On the one hand the reference to the sound of 'a woman being taken against her will' evokes the fear of rape, but simultaneously we see it is the white woman who has the power in this situation. She is the one in control and, as it emerges, has the power to determine the man's fate. As in *Holy Day*, Bovell is interested in testing the contradictions and tensions inherent in the role of the white woman under colonialism: in gender terms she is vulnerable and yet in racial terms her 'whiteness' gives her an assumed superiority. Thus, her 'right' to be here is unquestioned, while his right is not even a consideration. Indeed, she tells him he has no right to be on her land and she tells him something of her history; how her grandfather had 'opened up this country'. Her grandfather was a resourceful pioneer who had: 'built his own house. Just from what was at hand. And not just a shack ... But a house made of stone. Made to last ... And the furniture. He made all the furniture. Tables. Chairs. Beds ... He made that chair' (2002b:6) – and here she points out an armchair made with the cured hides of animals. She tells the man a familiar story of the indomitable colonial spirit; the ethos of 'making do', the value of hard work and determination to succeed against tremendous odds. In the light of this history she tells him: 'It gets into your blood, this country. It comes to be part of you. So who are you to trespass? Who are you to look at me?' (2002b:7). Her insistence on her rights above his, which include her right not to be looked at by him, are part of her assumed white privilege.

The woman says she has sent word to the authorities who will come and collect the man by morning but it is clear that he would rather die than be taken into captivity, and he begs the woman to let him go. In a bargain that recalls the ancient Scheherazade legend, the woman agrees to let him go if he can tell her a story that will move her as she feels 'like my heart has turned to stone ... like my blood has stopped flowing within me ... like my skin would break if it were touched' (2002b:7) The man tells a story of his people's dispossession and destruction, and of how 'the men on horses hunted plenty of them down, rounded them up and marched them back. And they shut them up in a pen, like they were cattle and then shot them. Then they took their skins and threw their bodies in a pile and set it alight. And they used those skins to cover their furniture'. Hearing this horrendous tale and seeing the unmistakable connection between her story and his, the woman lets him go and sets fire to the chair. While the act of destroying the chair could be seen to be redemptive, Bovell does not let the audience off the hook. The man escapes into the night but he is heading for certain death and so it is but a momentary reprieve. The audience is left with a powerful sense of dramatic irony – knowing with the wisdom of hindsight that the legacy of colonialism for Aboriginal people continues, to the present day, to tell a largely tragic story.

In this short play, a number of ideas are at work. Bovell is once again focusing our gaze on colonial history and the violence and destruction meted out by the colonists to the Aboriginal people. As in *Holy Day*, Bovell is interested in exploring the contradictions between, on the one hand, the taken-for-granted associations of white society with the forces of 'civilisation', and on the other, the actual histories of genocide and abuse. The woman's account of the courage, independence and skill with which her grandfather settled the land connotes Howard's portrayal of Australia's past as one of 'heroic achievement'. But the story told within the play which tells of Aborigines being systematically murdered and then flayed so that their skins might be used to make furniture is one that must deconstruct the hegemonic view of white Australia's history being marked by acts of heroism such that current generations will regard it with pride. Bovell says: 'Perhaps we read that the piece is about the contradiction between the black narrative and the white narrative; what [does] the chair stand for, whose history does it represent?' (Bovell 2002a).

Further, it is interesting to note that the white woman in *The Chair* makes the man's freedom contingent on his being able to tell her a moving story, a story that will stir her emotions. Helen Thomson noted in her review that the play 'chillingly suggests that the murder and dispossession of Aborigines has as little power to touch the emotions of present-day whites as it did when the atrocities occurred' (Thomson 2002). This is confirmed by Bovell when he says: 'What I'm questioning are matters to do with the inability of white people to be truly moved by the Indigenous story and the packaging of the Indigenous story for white consumption' (Bovell 2002a). This idea that white Australians are, to some extent, inured to stories of Indigenous suffering helps underscore Bovell's choice of such a shocking and visceral story at the heart of this play – a story which can be read in terms of its multiple connotations of ethnic cleansing and the holocaust. Bovell goes on to point out: 'for us as white people stories of the stolen generation, stories of dispossession, stories of massacre and genocide are meaningless to us, as meaningless as they have always been' (Bovell 2002a). Bovell provokes contemporary audiences by producing a resolutely unredemptive picture of the relationships between white and Aboriginal Australia. As he himself puts it, this is 'a fairly despairing thing to say, but a provocative position to put' (Bovell 2002a). As these plays demonstrate, he refuses to paint a picture of false hope – and in this sense, Bovell's thinking is in line with Ghassan Hage's argument about the ways in which fear of the 'other' has produced a national sense of disillusionment.

Both *Holy Day* and *The Chair* make an important contribution to the 'genre' of writing about Indigenous issues from the perspective of a non-Indigenous playwright. The plays are distinctive for their critique of a triumphalist reading of Australia's past and their repudiation of the conventional national history of colonial achievement; history which tells a one-nation story while eliding a two-nation reality. A further distinctive feature is the focus on whiteness. Rather than telling the story of an Indigenous person as an object or victim of white society, the play interrogates the ways in which whiteness gives structural advantage and race privilege. This involves making apparent the otherwise masked operations of white power. To this end, Bovell works in two ways: first, he sets up a complex political/ideological environment within which his white protagonists exercise their power. The white women at the centre of the drama exercise power over the Indigenous characters, and we see how whiteness is inflected with and negotiated through their gender and class. Secondly, Bovell challenges the assumed and unspoken relationship between whiteness and 'normality' or 'civilisation'. Thus, Bovell's work does not simply repudiate the dominant reading of Australia's heroic past but provides a political deconstruction of power relations which continue to be relevant in the here and now.

Wonderlands

I believe people have this incredible capacity to change ... and
I believe people will have the capacity to deal with horrors if
they are allowed to see what they are actually dealing with
(Thomson 2005a)

Katherine Thomson's play is written in the wake of the debates around
land rights which emerged after the *Wik* decision in 1996. The play
was commissioned and produced in 2003 at the HotHouse Theatre
Company in Albury–Wodonga followed by a season at the Stables
Theatre in Sydney, directed by Marion Potts. It explores aspects of
land rights and its connection to a sense of identity and belonging from
the perspective of Indigenous and non-Indigenous characters, and
presents the issue of land rights from multiple perspectives. Like Bovell,
Thomson identifies and understands the role of history in determining
contemporary attitudes and beliefs. And as in *Holy Day*, *Wonderlands*
shows how contemporary certainties are often forged out of histories
which are partial and certainly not disinterested. In *Wonderlands*,
there is a history which is actively silenced in order to protect the
status quo. Thomson, like Bovell, acknowledges and counts the cost
of hidden truths about what happens to a community which does not
know its own history and which suppresses the unsavoury aspects of
the past. At the same time, Thomson and Bovell themselves participate
in the creation of partial histories; their plays are polemical in that
they are political and intended to affect the attitudes of audiences.
By constructing a critique of hegemonic colonial histories and the
polemic which attends them, they are themselves producing another
version of the past, with its own claims to truth, and its own political
agenda. In a sense then, Thomson and Bovell are operating within the
same paradigm that they are seeking to deconstruct. Nevertheless,
as they train their critical eye on the legacies of British colonisation,
these historical dramas produce a reading of white Australia which
destabilises dominant political discourse.

Historian Henry Reynolds, in his introduction to *Wonderlands*,
sees the play as making a significant contribution to the land rights
debate subsequent to the *Wik* Decision which established that the
Pastoral Lease was 'an inferior form of land tenure' (Thomson 2004:

x). This decision outraged many pastoral and grazier families, but as Reynolds points out: 'the pastoralists of the 1990s had forgotten the brutal conflict that had so often accompanied the establishment of the pastoral industry and the critical role of Aboriginal labour once that conflict came to an end. The Aborigines had forgotten neither' (2004: x). This notion that non-Indigenous Australians wilfully forgot the past is taken up by the play in order to address the political consequences for contemporary audiences.

The play is set on a grazing property, Ambertrue, and moves between two time periods and two parallel plot lines. One story line is set in 1931 where Alice, a white grazier, has just inherited Ambertrue, passed on to her from her parents who settled the place in the mid-1880s. The second story line is set in the present day and portrays the current white owners of Ambertrue, Lon and Cathy. Together the two stories are interwoven setting the context for the struggle over one piece of land. Like the country town, discussed in the next chapter, this piece of land acts at a metaphoric level to address the bigger question of Native Title and the way in which the land engenders a sense of national belonging for both Indigenous and non-Indigenous Australians. Thomson describes the original set for the play's production at the HotHouse Theatre as incorporating a 'packed red-earth floor' and a 'gumleaf-encrusted curtain snaking across the space' which was used to differentiate locations and distinguish between the acting areas (2004:xiv). These design elements reinforced the play's focus on the land itself, its physical as well as its metaphoric qualities. This was again reinforced at the play's end where 'the rear doors of the theatre opened and Edie and Cathy walked out together into the night, towards the actual trees and the river beyond' (2004:xiv). The combination of direction and design help to underwrite and focus the play's concern with the land as an 'actual' entity as well as a metaphorically significant site for both Indigenous and non-Indigenous Australians.

The story set in 1931 portrays Alice working alongside the Aboriginal stockman, Jim, who has lived on the property all his life, as did his father, mother and grandparents. Alice discovers journals kept by her father which describe how when he first came to the land 'the old blacks came to help' as he set up camp (2004:35). The journals are a device to introduce a third time period into the action – evoking an even earlier period of the colonial settlement of the area in the late nineteenth century. The journals, together with Alice's own affectionate memories of growing up on the property, make her determined to record the ancient (and rapidly disappearing) traditions and language of the local Yirralong people. Alice's written account of this history re-emerges seventy years later, in the present day, where the current white owners, Lon and his wife Cathy, are keen to suppress any historical facts about the original presence of the Yirralong on their land.

The present day action sees Lon and Cathy in a state of anxiety since their daughter Tessie, having agreed to marry her boyfriend and local farmer, Tom, has taken off into the city on the pretext of finding a wedding gown. Instead it seems that Tessie has run away leaving her fiancé in the lurch and crushing her father's hopes of passing the family holding on to his kith and kin. At the same time a local Aboriginal woman, Edie, and the Indigenous community are preparing to make a Native Title claim on behalf of the Yirralong people. The character of Edie sometimes takes on the role of narrator in this drama, acting as an interlocutor and introducing the audience to the history and political struggles of the Yirralong community. Here there is a battle on two fronts – within the community itself there is division about which of them are Yirralong people. And amongst the community of local white farmers, like Lon and Cathy, there is suspicion and fear about the potential for Native Title claims to take away their livelihoods. The journals of Lon's distant forebear, Alice, have the potential to reveal the truth about the validity of the Yirralong claims to Lon's property, but Lon is determined to erase this history at all costs.

In the figure of Edie and the relationship that is finally (though tentatively) brokered between her and Cathy, Thomson sees the redemptive potential of reconciliation. Her choice to have the Edie character act as narrator, a point of connection between black and white, is a structural device to reinforce her political point. This makes her play very different to Bovell's – in *Holy Day* the possibilities for redemption are more difficult to glimpse. But the two plays are linked by their belief in the ameliorative power of articulating what Thomson calls the 'dark secrets' of the past. Like Bovell, Thomson sees history as playing a critical role in determining our understanding of ourselves, and especially our national values. Thomson says: 'As a non-Aboriginal Australian I have no choice but to understand our history in all its inspiration and shame. If we've missed out on "being told", as we mostly have, then we're the losers if we don't make the effort to find out' (2004:xii). Where Bovell seeks to locate systemic racism in the paternalism and fear of difference manifested by those who colonised Australia, Thomson finds that there is something for contemporary audiences to learn from those pioneers who worked alongside, and in mutual relationships with, Aboriginal communities. One reviewer commented that the play is 'a lament for a lost opportunity for co-operation and mutual respect between white and black people on the land' (McCallum 2003).

In her notes to the play, Thomson seeks to contextualise and rationalise her approach by outlining the evidence in the historical record – evidence which suggests that not all white settlers and pastoralists discriminated against their local Aboriginal communities (2004:xii). Thomson found, for example, that in the late nineteenth century many squatters wrote letters to the Queensland newspapers expressing their horror 'of the violent frontier wars that were being conducted ... [and] their shame at the barbarity' (2004:xii). More particularly, Thomson found inspiration in the diaries of nineteenth century British settlers who established reciprocal exchanges with Aboriginal people. She gives the example of the Kemp family in rural Queensland who 'from their first arrival in the Channel Country [were] open to Aboriginal practice, tradition, knowledge, lore and law, and their lives were enriched accordingly' (2004:xii).

Following the evidence on the historical record, the main character, the pioneer Alice, decides to legally appoint the Aboriginal stockman Jim as the inheritor of the property in her will as a way of acknowledging both his family's original ties to the land and Jim's own lifelong husbanding of it. Alice's feelings about the reciprocal nature of her family's relationship with the local Aboriginal community are manifested in her commitment to recording their shared history. Thus, when she discovers her father's journals, she tells Jim: 'All I know is that this [the journal] puts us somewhere. My family. And yours. It's our history of our time together. We're part of this. A continuum. It's not my role – or your role – to stop that continuum now' (2004:37). But the continuum is indeed broken. Alice dies before she has a chance to sign over the land to Jim, and her cousin, Lon's distant forebear, inherits the land and passes it down through the generations to the present day where Lon and Cathy have become its owners. Lon refuses to believe (despite the evidence) that the Yirralong have any claims to the land his family has worked for 119 years. Terrified of the prospect of a Native Title claim on his farm, Lon attempts to destroy all the evidence of the historical associations of the Yirralong with the property. Lon repudiates the past which he feels is an encumbrance: 'Lugging history on your back's a sure-fire way to become a pain in the neck' (2004:16). While the Aboriginal woman, Edie, sees the past as a shared history between the local white and black communities, Lon is of the view that what happened in the past was a competitive struggle for resources, and he tells Edie there was a clear winner:

> You lost the first day people came up here. It was survival of the fittest and you lost. And we survived here. And it kills you. Your families are wrecks and your men bash you senseless and your livers are shot with the drink and you churn out the same old rubbish that the land talks to you or something ... you lost and you're very poor losers ... Now let's look to the future (2004:29).

Lon's social Darwinist justification reflects a similar philosophical view to the character of Wakefield in Bovell's play. For both Wakefield and Lon progress is inevitable and rational, and acts of racial violence and dispossession can be rationalised in its name. This is a compelling representation of the way in which whiteness confers superiority and racist doctrine comes to be seen as 'natural' and logical.

However, Thomson does not simply identify and target a racist 'type' for didactic purposes. As Reynolds argues in his introduction: '[the play] is not didactic: it doesn't preach and it isn't predictable'; rather it is peopled with 'autonomous and psychologically plausible characters' who are 'well grounded in time and place' (2004:ix). This is Thomson's 'great achievement ... She humanises an otherwise abstract struggle

over land and human rights and has turned it into compelling drama'
(2004:x). Thomson creates Lon as a complex individual whose passion
for his vocation as a farmer and the land he works on is intermixed
with his fear about the potential incursions of Native Title claims.
His anxiety about what he perceives to be the threat to his livelihood
is underpinned by a passionate connection to the land. He explains:
'Very few nights I haven't slept here … on this property … On the few
occasions I wasn't sleeping here I dreamt all night I was …' (2004:3).
Lon's dreaming of his land is perhaps intended to suggest a parallel
to the spiritual connection with which the 'dreaming' of Aboriginal
people locates them within a specific territory. Like Edie, Lon has a
profound attachment to the land: 'My boots aren't on the soil, they're
of the soil. Like those clouds scudding across that huge, awesome sky,
that country scuds through my veins. Pulsing like a bass guitar … I will
not have that taken away from me' (2004:48).

This sense of belonging is an inherited and familial quality, passed
down to Lon from his father who, when he had the property: 'felt like
he'd been handed an orphan. This land was orphaned … But he knew
he'd been called to set it right' (2004:3). Lon's sense of commitment
and obligation explains his near obsession with passing on the land to his
own daughter and her fiancé Tom: 'What I'm trying to say is that for me
to know that something's taken care of … that you're marrying Tessie,
you'll take over, that if I cark it suddenly I won't be leaving this place
orphaned' (2004:4). Thus, Thomson is suggesting, Lon's attachment
to the land has its own spiritual and familial connections, and this is a
key feature of the fight over land rights between the original owners
and the white pastoralists. The tragedy, perhaps, is the way in which
endemic racism (and the fear and paranoia which feeds it) prevents
white pastoralists from seeing the possibilities for reconciliation with
Aboriginal communities with whom they share a common interest, as
well as a shared history and mutual attachment to the land.

But Lon repudiates the lessons of history. He tells Edie: 'I don't
need a history lesson, thanks', to which Edie replies: 'It's *all* you need'
(2004:48). Lon refuses to see how he and his family have benefited
from the dispossession of the Yirralong, in his eyes it was a struggle
won by the 'naturally' superior and civilising forces of whiteness. And

the possessiveness which defines his attitude to the land also extends to his feelings towards his wife and daughter whom he sees as essentially extensions of his own will and desires. Cathy tells him: 'You think you know me. No, you think you possess me. Me and Tessie ... You claim us as yours. But that's not the same, Lon. As knowing' (2004:59). Thomson is suggesting that Lon's refusal to come to terms with the realities of the past, the dispossession of the original inhabitants of the land by his predecessors, is connected to his current emotional limitations. Thus, acknowledging and taking responsibility for the past is a feature of one's capacity to be honest in the present. The distinction Cathy makes between 'knowing' and 'claiming' is critical here. Lon claims the land because he has both a legal claim as well as a feeling of connection towards it; by implication, however, he does not 'know' the land in the same way that the original inhabitants did and do. The play suggests that it is Jim and his family and the Yirralong people whose claim to the land is based in their prior knowledge and their profound understanding of it.

In constructing this scenario for her drama, Thomson has gone to the heart of the tensions that exist between Indigenous and non-Indigenous Australians since the changes to native title legislation. As Judith Brett describes it, this debate is structured between: 'Indigenous people feeling a powerful sense of loss and dispossession; to non-Indigenous Australians such as miners, pastoralists and farmers feeling anxious about the possible expansion of native title rights, as well as those non-Indigenous Australians who felt suspicious about Indigenous people gaining special advantages on the basis of specious claims' (Brett 2002:198–9). Thomson's portrayal of Lon, and his battle with Edie as representative of the Yirralong people, catches many aspects of this debate; in particular the sense of loss experienced by contemporary Aborigines, and the anxiety and suspicion felt by white Australian farmers about the rightfulness of Indigenous claims to farming lands. That the play captured a significant public debate is confirmed by its reviews. One describes it as 'striking and vital' for its success in finding 'a more truthful drama inherent in the devastating effects of wearing a white blindfold' (Dunne 2003a). Another sees Thomson's play, along with Rayson's *Inheritance*, as part of a 'resurgence of the genre of rural dramas about black–white relations', and that such thematic explorations tell us that 'there seems to be unfinished business' (McCallum 2003b). This view is reinforced by Fensham and Varney who argue that both Thomson's and Rayson's plays were significant because they forced these issues 'into the cultural mainstream' (Fensham and Varney 2005:181).

These three plays — *Holy Day*, *The Chair* and *Wonderlands* — written in response to the reconciliation process reject the hegemonic discourses of much colonial history, with its emphasis on heroic struggle against adversity. The struggle is seen discursively in terms of nation building with the dispossession and destruction of Aboriginal peoples viewed as the unfortunate but inevitable consequences of the triumph of progress. It is precisely this view which informs the recent writing of the neo-conservative journalist Janet Albrechtson who argues that the teaching of Australian history should focus less on the notion of white invasion, and instead emphasise the contribution of British colonisation to 'civilised society [and] the rule of law' (Albrechtson 2006). These plays, on the other hand, point to the ways in which the hegemonic history advocated by Albrechtson remains silent about the systematic, invasive and violent nature of colonialism. Thomson says about the writing of *Wonderlands*:

> I was consciously working against this idea that the 'black armband' version of history was holding us all down, I think it releases us. … We had these dark moments, these subterranean chains on us … so by articulating it, when you expose it to the air, it becomes less powerful, you scrape the mud off it, and it begins to evaporate, the dark secret, you acknowledge it and then it doesn't have that kind of power (Thomson 2005a).

The plays acknowledge the past in all its 'shame and inspiration'. They reveal the economic self interest that underpins the historic interactions between white and black Australians. In *Wonderlands*, Lon exclaims to Edie: 'I did not steal that land' to which she replies: 'Well, someone did and you reap the benefits' (2004:51). Both plays represent racism as not simply the acts of explicitly racist people – but see it as socially and economically determined, produced by people with complex motivations and attitudes, and often framed by the discourses of biology which see racial differences as immutable.

Further, these plays unravel some of the grounding assumptions of the ideology of 'whiteness' by questioning taken-for-granted ideas about the 'natural' equation of the 'white' with civilisation. The plays look at how 'whiteness' – the assumption of power and dominance by white society – produces an unacknowledged frame through which we understand and derive advantage from the status quo. This is what Stephenson calls the 'seeming normativity' of 'whiteness' and its 'structured invisibility' (Stephenson 1997). Bovell and Thomson make explicit and visible the nature of 'whiteness' as a political and social classification, so contributing to the current debates around both Indigenous land rights and the role of history in shaping the nature of racial relations in Australia. These plays by non-Indigenous writers are notable for the way they avoid explaining the past through a description of the experience of pre-colonial aboriginality – a task which Bovell insists is for Indigenous writers to capture. The work of Bovell and Thomson is an important development within Australian theatre writing traditions: rather than seeing racism as a problem affecting 'Others', here racism is seen and understood as something which is tied to the definition of 'whiteness' itself.

The ideas which underpin the theatre work of non-Indigenous writers are similar to those which inform the colonial histories undertaken by historians like Henry Reynolds who has written about the destruction of entire Indigenous communities which continued into the twentieth century (Reynolds 1981). Brett describes such work as producing 'a changed state of knowledge' about the past – a change which is not reflected in contemporary government policy (Brett 2002:202). For Brett, the policy of practical reconciliation refuses to take on board the insights and concerns of those historians and commentators (and, one might add, the playwrights discussed here) who have attempted to reinterpret the colonial period (2002:202).

According to Brett it is an oversimplification to see Liberal government policies of practical reconciliation and the repudiation of the 'black armband' histories as racist. Rather, she argues: 'Howard and his ministers have simply refused to acknowledge the changed state of knowledge, and have formulated policy as if they were still in the 1960s and the only problem was one of securing equal citizenship for all Australians' (2002:202). Others put a strong argument for the importance of symbolic reconciliation; symbolic acts of acknowledgement about the wrongs of the past. Aileen Moreton-Robinson has argued that 'black armband' denotes mourning; 'or, as Indigenous people would say, "sorry business"' and that the black armband view of history is repudiated by the present government because it 'diminishes the nation's virtue' (2004:222). The plays discussed here take up some of this territory; they engage in the symbolic act of acknowledging the terrible realities of the past and in so doing lay bare the relationship between national history and national 'virtue'.

The importance of this relationship between history and morality is underscored by Poole:

> A national identity involves, not just a sense of place, but a sense of history. The history constitutes the national memory, and it provides a way of locating those who share that identity within an historical community. The history is not given, but subject to debate and reinterpretation … Australian history is now coming to terms with the suffering, destruction and human tragedy consequent upon the European settlement of Australia. The details of this history may be debated, but it cannot be disavowed. Acquiring a national identity is a way of acquiring that history and the rights and responsibilities which go with it. The responsibility to come to terms with the Australian past is a morally inescapable component of what it is to be Australian (1999:140).

The plays discussed here are intimately concerned with the debate and reinterpretation of history, and they understand the critical relationship between national identity and national memory. Further, they demonstrate how contemporary political theatre in Australia takes on the hard issues of the moral obligations and responsibilities of national identity. The relationship between race, national history and national identity is a contested site where the ideological implications of nationalism are being fought out. Howard has promoted a version of the past which emphasises heroic achievement – a view that others (such as Albrechtson) seek to promulgate by reinforcing the civilising benefits of European colonisation. Bovell and Thomson have an oppositional view. Like many other non-Indigenous playwrights and screenwriters since the 1970s, Bovell and Thomson wish to write plays which invigorate the reconciliation process. Arguably, because of the derailment of reconciliation as a public and policy project, their task has been made more urgent in recent years and their work should be viewed in the light of these political circumstances. This is political theatre, not just because it is topical, but because it engages in current debate, in the teeth of opposition, and uses theatre as a forum to do so. This theatre practice manifests a critical approach to hegemonic nationalism and encapsulates Goldfarb's notion, of 'principled critical action' which he uses to define intellectual activity in the public sphere (1998). For Goldfarb this intellectual activity is not just to be found in the work of the 'public scholar or scientist', but also in the work of artists 'with public concerns' (1998:103). Bovell and Thomson fit this bill; for them the theatre is a platform for telling dramatic stories which speak directly to the key issues on the national agenda. Their plays are principled, critical, and informed by their professional skill in the creation of emotionally powerful stories that speak to contemporary audiences.

These plays make a significant contribution to the critical nationalist approach: they repudiate the triumphalist versions of Australia's history which emphasise colonial achievement rather than acknowledging the histories of Indigenous experience under colonialism. As Helen Thomson has described it, these works underline 'the stage's unique ability to provide a place for the spoken voice to answer, in public, the denials of Aboriginal experience in Australia's post-contact history contained within the pro-Windschuttle historical polemics' (Thomson, H. 2004:141).

Steve Bisley as Lyle in the 2003 Melbourne Theatre Company production of *Inheritance*. (Photo: Jeff Busby)

CHAPTER 3

THE POLITICS OF PLACE

'The truthful production of a playwright's voice and vision enriches the nation' **Ben Ellis** (2004).

Rural Australia

The representation of the Australian countryside and the country town are familiar tropes in Australian culture. While Australian cinema has provided some of our most enduring images of landscape, the theatre has also provided opportunities for its largely urban audiences to engage with the worlds outside the cities. The representation of rural Australia was a persistent feature of both the pre- and post-Federation theatre. Such representations became 'convenient emblems' for the nation and provided evidence for the perception of 'national distinctiveness' (Wolf 2004:6). The portrayal of fires and floods, the characters of the diggings and the bush characterised much of Australia's nineteenth-century drama. Bucolic melodramas used 'bush beauty spots' along with 'a genial bushman or digger' to evoke the particularities of life in the new world (Williams 1983:116). Later, more literary plays by writers such as Louis Esson (*Dead Timber* first performed in 1911 and *The Drovers* in 1923) and Steele Rudd (*On Our Selection* first performed in 1912) established emblematic bush characters recognisable for their 'terse matter-of-factness and dislike of emotional display ... men not given to easy words, embarrassed by a drastic event, the sudden loss of one of their mates' (Rees 1978:134). The taciturn Australian bushman is also a feature of Ray Lawler's *Summer of the Seventeenth Doll* (1955). In this canonical 1950s drama the setting is domestic and urban, but the bushman stereotype is clearly in view. Indeed, as Peter

Fitzpatrick points out, the iconic figure and 'the nature of the myth of the bushman and the doctrine of mateship' is the primary subject of Lawler's drama (Fitzpatrick 1979:11).

In more recent times the pastoral drama faded from view although the cultural resonances of its iconography were conjured in the period films of the 1970s. One of the most critically successful Australian films from the 1970s was *Sunday Too Far Away* (1975) directed by Ken Hannam. Set on a sheep shearing station in the 1950s, it is a political film which addresses such issues as unionism, strike breaking, the scourge of non-union labour, and the class-based struggles of the shearers versus the wool graziers. With its laconic sense of humour, its approving nod towards the moral values of the hard-working shearers, and its nostalgic rendering of mateship, egalitarianism and the fair go, the film is an exemplar of the 'new nationalist' ethos of the 1970s.

By comparison, the theatre of the New Wave was not interested in reproducing sentimental images of the rural environment: Jack Hibberd's *Dimboola* (1969), for example, used 'comic-strip absurdity' to paint a picture of a country wedding (Williams 1983:210). On the other hand, plays like David Williamson's *Don's Party* (1971) bespoke the New Wave's interest in the critique of suburbia and its values. An exception from the 1970s was Dorothy Hewett's *The Man from Mukinupin* (1979) set in the 1920s in a mythical country town in the wheatbelt of Western Australia. Mukinupin, one critic noted, was 'one of those parched outback townships etched on the Australian race memory' (Radic 1991:209). While the play acknowledges the 'black stain of genocide' it is nonetheless a largely affectionate look at life in a country town. In her foreword to the play, Katharine Brisbane notes that Hewett's 'celebration of country life' is 'full of tribal memory' (Brisbane 1979:vii). In this sense the play underwrites the perception that country life and values are of historic and 'tribal' significance within Australian culture.

This chapter focuses on four major plays produced between 1998 and 2003 that are set outside the cities. They not only rethink the iconography of the Australian countryside, but also interrogate its putative tribal significance. These plays are significant for two reasons: first, they were written in response to changes within the political and economic sphere. Secondly, by critically addressing the familiar iconography of the outback and the country town, these writers re-read the nation in order to present a countervailing discourse on nationhood and Australian-ness.

The four plays are *Inheritance* (2003) by Hannie Rayson, *Falling Petals* (2003) by Ben Ellis, *Navigating* (1997) by Katherine Thomson, and *Last Cab to Darwin* (2003) by Reg Cribb. While they vary in style and tone, they have common characteristics. They represent a deconstruction of the Australian legend with its essentialist mythologies of the bush as the nation's moral heartland. At the same time, they (re)capture some idea of the 'ordinary' Australian. The characters in these plays live lives of unending struggle – a struggle that is produced by physical and political hardship. A cursory glance might suggest that these plays represent the continuation of an older typology of the so-called 'Australian Legend' – Russel Ward's (1966) hard working 'Aussie' battler, tough and admirable. But rather than reproducing an existing set of understandings about national identity, these plays subject received wisdoms to critical scrutiny by testing their underlying assumptions. For example, playwright Ben Ellis describes his impetus to write the play *Falling Petals* as coming from his sense that 'the bush or the rural town is seen ... as representing Australia in the national imagination':

> I was always conscious of Australians being [an] extremely urbanised nation and ... I almost feel a sense of grievance that people would make the bush the repository of all Australian qualities ... without knowing anything about what it's like to actually live there. I wanted to exploit that certainty about the town being the repository of Australian goodness ... I wanted to use young characters who were intelligent ... and involve them in discussions about power and economics which are ... crippling their lives (Ellis 2005).

Ellis and the other playwrights acknowledge the 'realities' of rural life and the characteristics of those who live it, and simultaneously deconstruct its ideological potency. This is made possible by the nature of the legend itself which, as Richard Nile describes it, 'appears to be both "real" and "representative"' (Nile 2000:2). These plays portray the 'ordinary' Australian as both real and representative, and in this way the 'category' itself can be understood as both a fact about rural life, *and* as an ideological construction.

In his analysis of the impact of the past twenty years of economic reforms on Australians, Michael Pusey argues that it is vital to understand the relationship between changes in the economic and political landscape, and lived experience. How have people's family and working lives been changed, he asks, and what are the ongoing social repercussions of these changes? Pusey says that we need to understand how economic reform 'has reshaped our dispositions and orientations towards each other ... how it challenges our practical moralities, our trust in others, our time horizons, our coping strategies, and our sense of where we fit in the larger society' (2003:xiii). The plays under consideration here similarly consider the social changes produced by economic reform. Like Pusey, the playwrights address issues such as morality and trust not simply between individuals, but within a national context. Many of the characters in these plays are struggling to understand and cope with their changing social status. These plays provide an examination of the question of where Australians – particularly rural Australians – fit into the bigger political and social picture, and provide a critical view of the nation shaped by the forces of globalisation.

Two Nations

Throughout the 1990s the widening division between country and urban Australia became a significant political issue. Geographic inequalities were manifested in rural areas by increasing levels of unemployment, a low level of average income for those who had work, and the marked shift of population from country towns to the cities. Robert Manne argues: 'In the era of globalization, contemporary capitalism has developed a rather ruthless tendency to sort people out ... the winners are congregating in the inner city and its suburbs. The losers are collecting on the fringes of the cities and ... in the small or medium-sized country towns' (2001:165).

Manne explains the gradual decline in prosperity for the rural sector: the revenues from family farms diminished and the decline of agriculture meant that country towns struggled to survive. Further, he argues, the tide of economic rationalism brought privatisation; services to the rural sector, once underwritten by government subsidy, were now rationalised by private companies thus breaking the 'implicit social contract on which this country was built' (2001:166). The 1990s saw a shift of social, health and financial services to the larger regional centres and away from small country towns. Over a three year period, Manne points out, the Victorian country town of Moe 'lost its Medicare office, its local council, the Gas and Fuel and State Electricity Commission offices, water board ... for small towns the loss of services and the employment they provide can be terminal ...' (2001:166). It was into this economic and political environment that Pauline Hanson and the One Nation Party came to prominence. Hanson was elected as an independent to the Queensland seat of Oxley in 1996 and her party, One Nation, won nearly 23 per cent of the vote in the 1998 Queensland State election – a result which surprised the major parties. Hanson and One Nation promoted policies which sought to restrict immigration, repeal the *Native Title Act*, and reintroduce protective tariffs to favour primary producers. As Marilyn Lake describes it, when speaking for 'Australians' Hanson was primarily addressing herself to 'marginalised, rural, white Australian men – tapping into their persuasive sense of loss' (Lake 1998:118). Her rise to power was facilitated by a combination of anti-political cynicism and deep-seated xenophobia.

While it would appear that Hanson and the One Nation Party are now a spent force, these plays emphasise their political legacy and cost to the nation. McKnight argues, for example, that John Howard has 'continued to address the moral anxiety' of many Australians and has thereby 'largely recaptured the One Nation vote for the mainstream Right' (2005:11). Guy Rundle sees Hanson and Howard sharing a fundamental view about the importance of racial and cultural homogeneity and argues that this 'accorded with the view of an essentially Australian character on which Howard's values [are] grounded' (2001:26). These essentialist values about Australia and Australian-ness are part of the 'common sense' ideas which have won votes and helped to shape the ideological terrain. Indeed, the attempt to capture the idea of the 'ordinary' Australian is a key feature of the way these plays work against the grain in terms of prevailing political ideas about national identity. John Howard, the 'self-proclaimed "Average Australian"', consistently identified the cultural importance of key national values including mateship, egalitarianism and respect for the nuclear family unit. This, then, is the political and ideological context which informed the four plays under consideration here.

Inheritance

Hannie Rayson's play, directed by Simon Phillips, had its premiere at the MTC in March 2003 and played at the STC in April–May of that year. Rayson has a long-standing interest in writing drama based on field research, and this play was informed by the author's research trips to the Mallee in Victoria where she interviewed farmers and others in the region. Focusing on the specific issues facing rural workers and their families, Rayson interrogates the political sphere as it shapes people's values and beliefs. In the process of doing so audiences may find themselves questioning what Said calls the 'merciless logic' of political power (2002:32). In *Life After George*, Rayson looked at the corporatisation of the universities and the concomitant clash between the goals of a liberal education on the one hand, and the pursuit of the bottom line on the other. In this play, Rayson looks at the land, the environment of rural Australia, and asks: to whom does it belong?

Inheritance is a story of two families battling it out in the Mallee. The elderly twin sisters, Dibs Hamilton and Girlie Delaney, represent two kinds of rural family story. Dibs inherited the family farm and prospered; her children, Julia and William, are well-educated city folk and her adopted Aboriginal son, Nugget, is a successful farmer managing the family farm. Girlie, on the other hand, has had a tougher ride. Her son Lyle and his wife Maureen are embittered by their experience of life on the farm as one of endless struggle. This group of characters gathers together to thrash out the question of who will inherit Allandale, the family farm. Written in a series of short scenes, the play has a large cast with eleven main roles, and runs through different time periods: the present-day action is contextualised by historical scenes displaying the Delaney family's long-standing association with Allendale. The play moves through multiple settings, representing both internal and external locations, and establishing each family group in their domestic territories. In this way, a complex world of inter-connected relationships in the past and present is established. Together, these temporal and spatial juxtapositions help build the idea that the 'farm' has both a literal and metaphorical connotation. The 'farm' is a literal space, but it is also a synecdoche for the 'nation'. At the same time, the play addresses cultural assumptions about the country and the people who live there. The unexamined bush nostalgia and the celebration of earthy Australian values it supposedly engenders are repudiated through the drama. The essentialist view of the matey, self-reliant, fair-go Australian is revealed as a rationalisation of an altogether more malevolent intolerance of the outsider. This preoccupation links *Inheritance* to Rayson's other plays in the sense that they are all concerned to explore the point at which dominant ideas meet lived experience.

The play has its genesis in a critical enquiry about the currency of 'political correctness' as a strategy for creating consent and tacit approval; it questions the appeal and political successes of One Nation, and the way Hanson's rise to power had managed to produce (and was itself produced by) a great divide in the population. There were the rural 'rednecks' and the urban elites, and the two worlds missed each other by a country mile. Rayson comments:

> The sort of rhetoric that both sides were using was at a terrible despairing impasse, that was how I experienced it … Like most people in my particular circle … I was furious and frustrated by Pauline Hanson and her escalating power base and so there was really no alternative for me but to go and find out where that support was coming from, rather than simply saying: those people must be a sandwich short of a picnic (Rayson 2003a).

In order to move beyond the 'despairing impasse', Rayson's play does not represent the debate as a dichotomy between city and country. Rather, Rayson is concerned to create a familiar world made up of characters and scenarios which are readily identifiable, but complex and contradictory at the same time; audiences are encouraged to feel a connection to the characters, to their hopes and aspirations, while also being aware of the moral implications of their actions and silences. This interplay of familiarity (the use of recognisable characters, scenarios and idiom) with the objective of challenging received ideas is characteristic of Rayson's efforts to produce theatre in which audiences are encouraged to reconsider their ideas and beliefs.

In an attempt to create a complex and dynamic dramatic experience, a key dramaturgical strategy is the use of contradiction. In a scene with her sister Girlie, Dibs reveals her attitudes towards her adopted son Nugget. Girlie asks her why she took him on rather than leaving him to be brought up by his Aboriginal mother, and Dibs replies: 'They couldn't look after him like we could. He had a proper home here and proper schooling' (2003b:86). Later in the scene Dibs rejects the idea that Nugget, as Farley's illegitimate son, might inherit the farm:

> I'm buggered if I'm going to honour his bloody dying wishes. I kept Farley's secret for thirty-eight years ... I stood by him all that time-and then he goes and does this. He expects me to hand over my family farm to his bastard son ... I am not giving Nugget a single handful of this dirt (2003b:86).

The scene is illustrative of Rayson's approach. On the one hand Dibs is revealed to be a Christian woman who believes in doing the right thing. In adopting Nugget as her son, and in standing by her unfaithful husband, she is certain that she is fulfilling her moral responsibilities. On the other hand, it becomes apparent that Dibs is capable of terrible moral perfidy rationalised by her unexamined racism. By creating characters who manifest contradictory beliefs and values, Rayson's plays explore the spectrum of moral ambiguity. Rayson notes:

> When I say my work is character-driven it means that the plays are always peopled with characters who contain huge contradictions, as do we all, and I am always interested in their having surprising kinds of qualities. People who are ruthless bastards in the board room are very charming at dinner parties, and people who work for the UN or help sink wells in Borneo can be extremely nasty to their own mothers ... the characters themselves have to contain multitudes ... I think that's also in itself a kind of politicizing idea – that people are capable of multiple thinking, and they can often sit with contradictory world views (Rayson 2003a).

The dramaturgical emphasis on contradiction emerges most clearly in *Inheritance* as it plays out an intensely personal drama against a particular socio-political context. One defines and articulates the other. The personal, familial drama of the Hamiltons and the Delaneys has a tragic resonance precisely because we understand these people's story within the framework of colonialism, globalisation and endemic racism. This is reflected in the story of Nugget's adoption by the Hamiltons whose treatment of their Aboriginal son is marked by a mixture of ignorance, repression, silence and guilt, all thinly papered-over by good intentions. Nugget's story of dispossession speaks to Australia's white history and to Rayson's understanding of the importance of acknowledging a racist past and its continuing legacy.

> One of the major themes in this play is about the white silencing of our history, and how that has completely … disempowered Aboriginal people. I wanted to show that … and ram it home. We see that the rug is pulled from underneath Nugget and he is left without anything, and yet the father is still saying to him that some things are best left unsaid, and it's impossible to shift the deadening oppressive hand of keeping things secret. We are not speaking the truth about what has happened because of white guilt from having colluded in the oppression in the past (Rayson 2003a).

This reflexive reading of the personal with the political defines Rayson's work; her plays are committed to the idea that theatre should express politics as lived experience, and vice versa:

> [My plays] are entirely about bridging the public and the private, about trying to deal with private moments in the stories of people's lives set against the historical, social and political backdrop. Politics exists and is manifested in how we live. My task as a dramatist is to make the recognisable and the particular and the known shed light on the bigger canvas. People think about politics as being quite separate from the way they live their lives, and my entire raison d'être is to bring the two things together (Rayson 2003a).

Along with its political edge, Rayson inflects her play with humour, and like her other plays, the tragic and the ironic are intermingled, one in dialogue with the other:

> GIRLIE: They're thieves, those Greeks!
> MAUREEN: Girlie!

GIRLIE: Blow-ins. And they don't pay tax neither. Who do they think
    pays for the roads and the schools and that?
MAUREEN: Their boy put in a good game in the ruck last Saturday.
GIRLIE: Still a wog.
MAUREEN: I hear young Felix has got himself a new girlfriend.
    Japanese.
GIRLIE: Oh, Christ All-Bloody-Mighty.
MAUREEN: I thought he was a homo (2003b:15).

The small-mindedness of these characters makes them feel certain
of their superiority, but marks them out as suspicious and intolerant.
By implication, this is the irony and tragedy of the country town; a
place, Rayson suggests, that is unable to change and grow because of
the intolerance of change and difference. Irony works at many levels in
the play: just as Dibs and Girlie settle the question of inheritance, Lyle
violently self-destructs; Maureen's political rhetoric about helping the
man on the land turns out to be a matter of political expedience when,
at the play's close, she happily turfs them all off the farm to finance
her personal ambitions.

The play's irony works to challenge nostalgic and utopian ideas
about the country and the people who live there. The play offers a
reworking of the iconic and romanticised view of the bush, a view that
has emerged through nineteenth-century art and literature, and more
recently was reiterated in the period films of the Australian cinema in
the 1970 and 1980s. Some of this familiar iconography is also present
in Rayson's play. In the opening scene of the Melbourne production,
for example, the production design highlighted a rusty red water tank
silhouetted against the sunset; a visual trope that immediately signalled
a familiar and iconic setting for the drama that follows. However, there
is much in *Inheritance* to suggest that nostalgia for the Australian bush
is misplaced; it is not, and has never been, a place of great moral virtue
but a very dark place indeed; a place of tragedies and repressions.
Further, the play asserts, this self-inflicted violence is historically
patterned, each generation seeming doomed to repeat it. In addition
to this re-reading of the aesthetic and iconic place of the country in
the public imagination, the play also provides a critique of a political
system which abandoned the rural sector, making country towns

unviable without basic services. In this way, the play also makes an argument about the rise of Hansonism; the politics of fear and blame is an inevitable consequence of economic circumstances in which people feel alienated and despairing about their capacities to affect change.

The critical reception to the play acknowledged Rayson's political concerns. Ball noted, for example, that that play 'is relevant to our times and will speak to different and competing audiences in a way that politicians can only dream of' (Ball 2003). The critic notes the breadth of Rayson's political interests in this play: 'women's property rights, gender identity ... city vs. bush, grassroots politics and ... Aboriginal land rights' (Ball 2003). Thomson, the *Age* theatre critic, also noted the way the play 'reveals the relentless realities – economic, political, climatic – that are undermining a frequently idealised way of life' (Thomson 2003). Herbert in the *Herald Sun* pointed to the potential political impact of the play when she comments that it 'reveals issues of rural life we might never consider in the city' (Herbert 2003a). Rayson has been criticised for writing 'issue' plays: *Inheritance* was described by Thomson, for example, as 'an almost complete inventory of rural woes' (Thomson 2003). In a similar vein, Wright has argued that Rayson's work is limited by its approach; it is old fashioned and overly concerned with the discussion of 'rational issues' (Prior 2003). Rayson disagrees and argues that rather than writing about issues for their own sake, her goal is to create drama which stirs debate:

> I try to be as surprising and unpredictable as possible because that's the stuff of the drama. So you are not just seeing some sort of values clarification exercise, or illumination of a moral fable, or an inventory of 'issues'. Hopefully, you are so embroiled in the story and captivated by the characters, it is only the next morning over breakfast that certain 'issues' take shape in your mind and open themselves for further consideration (Rayson 2003a).

Rayson's political theatre practice is defined by its responsiveness to topical and contemporary issues, while at the same time using a dramaturgy based on the construction of complex and contradictory characters to make those issues dense and provocative.

Rayson uses the rural setting as a means of discussing the state of the nation. The dry, understated humour of the play, coupled with the affection the writer clearly feels for the characters, might suggest that the work takes a celebratory approach to the portrait of Australians on the land. But the play constructs a more complex picture in which the virtues of mateship and the fair-go are interrogated and problematised. In particular, the play's insistence that the land, and by extension the nation as a whole, can be read as a locus for intolerance and fear of difference underscores the play's contribution to a critical reading of nationalism.

Falling Petals

Like Rayson, playwright Ben Ellis addresses the economic and political downturn of the rural sector. Ellis' own upbringing in the country meant that he witnessed 'the withdrawal of services from country areas and watch[ed] the economies of these places really free fall, things like the Pyramid Society collapse, and banks going, and teachers being knocked off two or three a year' (Ellis 2005). And while *Inheritance* concerns itself with generational disputes in relation to the control of the land, Ellis' play *Falling Petals* (2003) explicitly focuses on young people's experiences in rural Australia. Ellis thinks of generational issues and inter-generational politics as a key for understanding social divisions within Australia. Indeed, Ellis is one of a new generation of Australian playwrights who explores political subject matters, and his writing is informed by topical political and social issues. Unlike Rayson, Ellis does not set up a strictly naturalistic scenario, and instead takes audiences into a dark world notable for the almost complete absence of any redemptive liberalism. Ellis sees this as the distinctive feature of his work in the context of post-1970s Australian playwriting. He claims that he and other writers of his generation are 'following darker social worlds' (Safe 2002:17). There is no doubt that *Falling Petals* takes up this terrain, variously described by critics as: dark 'sci-fi satire' (Safe 2003:14), and 'biliously nasty satire' which by comparison makes 'Ionesco's *Rhinoceros* seem kind' (Marshall 2003:7).

Falling Petals premiered at the Playbox Theatre in Melbourne in June 2003, directed by Tom Healey, and was produced at Sydney's New Theatre in Newtown, directed by Mark Armstrong. It is set in the fictional town of Hollow which the author describes as 'rural suburbia' with a declining population of just over 10,000 people (Ellis 2003:1). The set features a cherry blossom tree, gradually losing its blossoms, around which most of the action takes place. Three friends, Tania, Sally and Phil, are in their final year of school and are hoping that they will get good enough results to get to university in the city. They are desperate to escape Hollow, a town which Phil describes as: 'small and nasty and fucked' (2003:3). Despite their ambitions, Mr. Syme, the careers guidance teacher who does not believe in giving them false hope, routinely discourages the students from setting their sights too high or aiming beyond local TAFE courses.

But it is not only the lack of ambition and opportunities in this small town that Phil and his friends want to run away from. The young children of Hollow are dying of a mysterious illness which builds to epidemic proportions. Only children are affected, starting with the very young and then gradually killing off older school children until the teenagers themselves fall prey to the 'child ridding disease' (2003:14).

The play is savage in its critique of an older generation which has disenfranchised and marginalised the young. In this sense *Falling Petals* shares some similar themes with Ellis' earlier play, *Post Felicity*, in which generational differences make it seemingly impossible for the parents to make any sense of, or even find an emotional connection with, the suicide of their daughter (Ellis 2002). In *Post Felicity*, Ellis explores an emotional numbness which the older generation has towards young people; a numbness which makes it impossible for them to understand the suffering of their children. In *Falling Petals*, Ellis goes further: the young are not simply victims, but are also capable of cannibalising their own. On hearing that one of their class mates has died Tania and Phil find solace in their own survival:

> TANIA: You have one less rival for a university place.
> PHIL: Yes. Yes. You're right.
> TANIA: That's one less competitor you have to worry about.
> PHIL: Yes. Maybe more will get it.
> TANIA: We'll be fine … Only people like us will be left.
> PHIL: People who know what needs to be done (2003:37).

Tania and Phil are contemptuous of their sick and dying mates, feeling that this is a case of survival of the fittest, and that it is their (imagined) natural superiority which makes them destined to survive. Ellis suggests that while the young are disempowered by society, they are not themselves outside ideology. In an interview Ellis describes how this understanding came from his experience of growing up in a country town where young people: 'actually desire the centre so much so they try to become it more than the other people' (Ellis 2005). Indeed, the young people in Ellis' play do not want to reject society, they want to be taken up by it. They long to show the world how ready for it they are. This contradiction at the heart of this play makes it a politically challenging theatre piece. There are no easy heroes here, no one to let the audience off the hook; no middle-class altruism or humanistic epiphanies are allowed to save the day.

All the apparent 'virtues' of rural life are debunked; to these disaffected teenagers the countryside's sense of space is like 'outer space', and fresh air smells like 'diesel and cow shit' (2003:5). The traverse staging of the play in the Melbourne Playbox production added to the sense of distanciation with the action of the play framed by an elongated narrow space rather than an intimate domestic one. This contributed to the sense of a deconstructed community. In an interview about the play, Ellis declared: 'I'm fed up [with] the sentimentality towards country areas, a belief that people look out for each other [and] are really community-minded … I wanted to subvert that stereotype by dealing instead with what I see as a cordoning off of youth, hope and possibilities' (Safe 2003:14). Ellis deconstructs the 'stereotype' of the community-minded country town by portraying the rampant individualism and self-interest which reveals itself when the disease becomes an epidemic. The disease is described as one in which: 'the organs of the body stop working for the body' (2003:14). The description of an illness in which the organs work independently, not as interdependent entities in a system, suggest that this is a metaphoric reading of individualism as a spreading and contagious disease which, in the end, destroys society.

Ellis portrays something akin to a generational war. The older characters – parents, teachers, local councillors – are closed-minded and opportunistic. Mrs Woods, Sally's mother, runs a small shop and she insists it is Sally's duty to stay and help, despite Sally's academic potential. Further study costs too much and Mrs Woods feels there is no point in Sally keeping her options open because 'there are none' (2003:18). Later, as the epidemic spreads and teenagers start to fall victim to it, Mrs Woods throws Sally out of home because she might be bad for business. Even mothers, in this scenario, will sacrifice their children for the sake of economic survival.

Ellis targets his sharpest satirical attention on the local politicians. In his speech to the local city council, Mulvaney, President of the Hollow Chamber of Commerce, will only acknowledge what he euphemistically calls the 'health problem in this area', and his view of the town's tragedy is pragmatic. As a representative of those in power in the town, Mulvaney reveals a cynical interest in handling the 'spin' rather than searching for either causes or solutions.

> There is no reason to associate us with this problem ... Hollow is your average, fine, typical, relaxing, beautiful countryside town that you can still take the family to ... even with the drought, it still possesses a stirring and striking Australian landscape. Think, people, of Hollow as being like something out of *Seachange* but cheaper ... (2003:24).

The older generation is seen to avoid self reflection at all costs, or taking responsibility, or examining causes. The townsfolk seem only able to treat the symptoms of the disease without ever acknowledging that it is systemic. And the 'arriviste' city folk do not help either: hobby farmers, or rich people from the city who 'play' at being farmers, are scorned in the play, as are the hippies, like Phil's parents, who are escaping the city in order to seek alternative lifestyles in the country. In this country town (and by implication across the non-fictional country towns of Australia) minds are closed, expedience rules, fear of the unknown is pandemic and leads to moral bankruptcy.

Just as Ellis takes apart our sentimental attachment to the countryside, so too does he tear away the notion of the innocence of children. The young people of Hollow are as incapable of experiencing genuine empathy as are their elders. Ellis explains:

> I only really understood it when I read about the Ihk [African tribe studied by cultural anthropologist Turnbull] ... they could

only laugh when they [saw] someone else's distress ... I was on youth committees in Bairnsdale – just knowing that the people who would kick out their kids, like 14-year-olds or 9-year-olds in some cases and make them live under bridges were people who had these ideas about authority and that things should be done this way ... the worst-off people would become the worst people ... And take great pleasure in seeing other people go down. If you don't have much yourself there is not much pleasure in watching people go up, watching people go down is an extremely pleasurable feeling (Ellis 2005).

In *Falling Petals* this self-interested and anti-community sensibility is manifested by parents and authority figures, as well as by the younger generation who are the primary victims of this uncaring regime. Phil thinks the disease is deserved, and cynically ascribes the phenomenon of 'Hollow hicks keeling over' to 'some inbred thing going back generations' (2003:28). Phil's lack of humanity and empathy for the victims of the disease that eventually kills him, too, means that he is not just a victim of the system, but a manifestation of it. The three teenage characters are narrow in their political views, while at the same time recognising the stultifying conservatism of their parents and teachers who are 'stupid, One Nation-voting cocksuckers complain[ing] about money' (2003:21). In one of the play's most powerful scenes, Tania and Phil have sex while reciting to each other the principles of the marketplace economy. The teenagers are blind to the irony of clinging to the apparently unassailable logic of an economic system that has profoundly failed them, a belief which seems all the more bizarre and irrelevant in the face of the imminent collapse of their world. While Tania and Phil recognise that being young and from the country is a form of double jeopardy, they are nonetheless desperate to make it 'out there' in the very system that oppresses them.

The play's satirical edge emerges as Ellis demonstrates how ill-equipped the people of Hollow are to deal with the disaster that engulfs them. Both young and old alike mouth self-help platitudes in the vain belief that these might be helpful: 'every problem is an opportunity', (2003:47); the key to surviving is 'staying motivated, on top of your game, competitive' (2003:56). The self-help cant is, Ellis suggests, a means of blocking reality; a mechanism by which the individual is effectively de-politicised. And along with the individualistic discourses of self-help comes its corollary – blame. Here, the young are seen by others as deserving of this generational 'cleansing'. In the play's closing moments, a desperate and dying Sally appeals to Phil's mother Gayle who backs away saying: 'Don't ask me for anything. I told you. You kids brought it on yourselves' (2003:64). In this way, Ellis constructs a parable for Hansonism; the small country town, he suggests, is a haven for fear and mistrust; suspicion and scapegoating, and these propensities are exploitable by politicians like Hanson.

Falling Petals received a mixed critical reception. The theatre review for the *Australian* described the play as 'clever' for tackling issues such as 'the sickness of selfishness and the challenges facing rural youth' (On 2003a). The reviewer noted Ellis' interest in exploring generational divisions without sentimentalising either side: 'in Ellis' view teenagers are truculent animals ... [and] adults are patronising tyrants'. In this way the play manages to be 'tough, unsettling theatre that reaches for the jugular' (On 2003a). This praise for the play was not shared by the *Herald Sun* review which criticised it for its 'relentlessly dislikable' characters and for its style which 'flip-flops between realism, cartoon, social satire, parody and contemporary grotesque' (Herbert 2003b). A further article in the *Herald Sun* noted that two audience members at a performance of the play had walked out and 'angrily confronted audience management' (Gray 2003). The article quotes from interviews with Ben Ellis and the play's director Tom Healey who stated that the play 'is saying some very provocative things about the baby-boomer generation' and that, as such, it had the potential to make some audience members angry (Gray 2003). Ellis is quoted as saying that he resists the idea that 'characters should be likeable' and insists that his primary concern in writing the play was to 'illustrate a generational divide' and that older audience members (and critics) may find it uncomfortable to be confronted by (or reminded of) 'what it's like to be an angry adolescent' (Gray 2003).

Along with Ellis' portrayal of self-obsessed baby-boomers, his savage and critical take on the family and family values may have been a further cause for audiences to feel uncomfortable. One of the central planks of Howard's ideological rendering of Australian identity is related to the

Celia Ireland as Darcy and Noni Hazlehurst as Bea in the 1998 Sydney Theatre Company production of *Navigating*. (Photo: Tracey Schramm)

family as a core social unit (Brett 2003:185). *Falling Petals* repudiates this comforting notion by deconstructing the family. Here mothers and fathers abandon their children and, along with teachers, politicians and social workers, seek expedient solutions to their suffering. Family allegiances are quickly brushed aside in this dog eat dog world. Ellis' deconstruction of the family is a persistent theme in his plays: in *Post Felicity* a daughter has committed suicide in unknown circumstances and the parents appear to know nothing at all about her life. Rather, they cling on to their memories of their own radicalised youth in the 1960s and blame their daughter for what they imagine to be her lack of moral fibre. The play constructs the older generation with the same shocking emotional blankness which the older characters manifest in *Falling Petals*. Both plays refuse to see the family as a sanctuary or as a primary unit of moral or social good, and instead find that families, as a metaphor for the nation, are riven with despair and self interest.

Like Rayson, Ellis provides a critical re-reading of national myths, and constructs a picture of the nation as morally bankrupt and self-deceiving. Contemporary ideological discourse around notions of family and community are here deconstructed. Unlike Rayson, however, Ellis does not have a liberal humanist worldview. Ellis' is a more radical reading of the state of the nation and his play boldly takes up the mantle of 'un-Australian' as the hegemonic signifiers of Australian-ness are stripped bare in his work. Self reliance has become self interest and the social cement of the family is recast to tell a more sinister story about the capacity of the family, and therefore the nation, to exercise control and administer punishment. While Ellis' play reveals a different philosophical view to Rayson's, these works nonetheless share a critical reading and destabilising of the category of the 'nation'.

Navigating

Written and produced in 1997, Katherine Thomson's play pre-dates both *Inheritance* and *Falling Petals*. Like Rayson and Ellis, Thomson has focused her gaze on the struggling country town in order to shed light on the bigger political picture. *Navigating* is the third in a trilogy of plays; *Barmaids* (1991) and *Diving for Pearls* (1991) have each explored the impact of social change on small communities, and this theme is further explored in *Navigating*. Thomson, like Rayson, looks for the inter-relationships between the public and private spheres. In her plays we see politics, not in a narrow sense, as an external force, but rather as a process by which we try to make sense of the changing patterns of our working lives. In an interview Thomson says about herself: 'politics is personal; that is quite conscious. But it's not just an affectation; I am deeply affected on a daily basis by what is going on' (Thomson 2005a). For Thomson politics is inescapably intermixed with how we live and what we believe. She is interested in politics as a force that determines how power is negotiated within society, and her plays provide insights into how that negotiation takes place.

At the same time, Thomson is concerned with exploring difficult moral territory: what are the moral consequences of our actions, or inactions? She has a different take to Ellis who, in *Falling Petals* for example, has created an amoral universe; in his country town the moral order no longer defines and rationalises behaviour or beliefs. In Ellis' bleak vision, the young are disempowered by a world order which despises and blames them. By contrast, in Thomson's plays, the individual has the capacity to struggle against the system that oppresses them; here there is choice, and the possibility of change through agency. This is a function of Thomson's optimism: 'the moments which most affect me in life, and in the theatre, [are] when someone reaches out in some small way' (Thomson 2005a).

Navigating was first produced in 1997 by the Queensland Theatre Company, directed by Richard Wherrett, and it then transferred to the MTC. It was produced by the STC in 1998 in a production at the Playhouse directed by Marion Potts. In this play, Thomson draws our attention to a locale in which ordinary lives are impacted by global economic forces. Interviewed for this book, Thomson pointed out that her choice of a small country town as the setting for the play was partly in response to her interest in how 'ordinary' people have coped with the changes wrought by economic rationalism, and partly resulted from her dramaturgical processes which meant that: 'My starting place was the town [itself] of course … I can't start a play unless I know what place it is in … I wanted it to have that sort of claustrophobic sort of hot-house feel and a sort of spookiness to it … .and it suited me that everyone would know each other, that there was nowhere to hide' (Thomson 2005a).

Having established the setting, Thomson creates a dramatic scenario in which the effects of privatisation, outsourcing and downsizing, are scrutinised as the characters of the play scrabble to cope with their losses, or take advantage of the benefits. In this environment of winners and losers, Thomson asks, how should we behave; what is the moral framework which will help us determine the right thing to do? Posing such questions provides an insight into her big-picture political analysis of the nation. Just as the characters in the country town are faced with moral challenges as they deal with the economic viability of their world, so the nation must face the question of moral leadership in the face of economic rationalism.

Navigating is set in the small seaside town of Dunbar. The local Cullodin Shire Council is pleased to find that Dunbar is the ideal location for a privately run prison, and there are three companies vying for the contract. As the play opens, the local movers and shakers on the Dunbar Development Group, led by Peter Greig, are hosting a visit by representatives of the three companies. Ian Donnelly, the council's Finance Officer, is rubbing his hands together at the anticipated windfall. Then he is visited by Bea, a middle-aged woman working in the council's accounting department, who claims she has evidence that Greig has been receiving money from one of the competing companies. Donnelly is keen to persuade Bea that the future economic viability of the whole area is dependent on this deal going through, and he advises her to keep quiet. Bea however continues her campaign to bring the evidence of corruption to light. Along the way she is systematically isolated and humiliated, first by her colleagues at work, and then by family and friends who are, almost without exception, unsupportive of her quest to seek the truth. In this environment, it is fear and self-interest which dominate over truth and due process.

It is Thomson's skill to create a fictional world peopled by 'ordinary' characters, living unremarkable lives and struggling to make sense of social change. Bea is a deliberately 'ordinary' character – an un-heroic figure who does the right thing, but is bossy and self-righteous. Thomson's capacity to write powerful and believable characters in an unsentimental vein ensures that while we see Bea is courageous and just, we might also feel that she's too intense, too controlled by her *idée fixe*. Thomson says: 'they say you value the dissident because they tell you who you are, so dissidents are uncomfortable people to be around … it was terribly important that [Bea] wasn't a likeable hero' (Thomson 2005a). Thomson resists the temptation to idealise her protagonist who behaves in highly principled ways in an environment where morality has been stained. At the same time, Bea is portrayed as both vexed and vexing, principled and inflexible, fighting the good fight, but in a strident tone that we know will not win her any fans.

The play has a complex plot which interweaves three strands: one plot line concerns the tragic past of Bea and her sister Isola; a second plot line contains the present day action in Dunbar; and the third, and least developed plot, weaves in the story of Darcy, a marginal character who plays a key role in the play's final moments. *Navigating* is written in a completely different style from the more surreal and satirical *Falling Petals*. Its use of naturalistic conventions, linear narrative, and psychological plausibility makes the play closer in style and tone to Rayson's *Inheritance*. Both seek to tie the past to the present day, and both use an episodic structure to evoke multiple dramas in specific geographic locales. Both writers, too, begin with the image of the country community choir to lock in the relationship between country town life and community values – a relationship which both plays proceed to deconstruct. Despite the stylistic differences between *Navigating* and *Falling Petals* these two plays share a similar dramatic interest in portraying the processes of social corruption; the idea of moral pollution as an epidemic. Thomson and Ellis have chosen a country town as the setting in which to explore the dynamic by which moral transgression gradually seeps into a small community, and becomes normalised. *Falling Petals* has the bleaker perspective with everyone – victims and perpetrators – falling prey to the corruption. But in *Navigating*, Bea represents the terrible vulnerability of the sole character who stands outside society and breathes a different air. This is another of Thomson's achievements in this play: in the character of Bea, she portrays the gradual grinding down of the truth through systematic pressure applied by those with a vested interest in keeping the truth hidden. Bea is sent to Coventry by her co-workers and she is humiliated and threatened by various powerful entities. And as the pressure on her mounts, the more Bea (and others) questions her sanity. Ian assures her that her corruption and bribery theories are 'all in your mind, all in your mind' (1998:47). But in a world where corruption becomes the norm, where is sanity to be found? This again has its parallels with *Falling Petals*; in Ellis' play it is disease and for Thomson it is madness that provides a metaphoric way of portraying a social structure in decay.

Like Rayson, Thomson has created a world which is in jeopardy because of a terror of its own history. The characters in Dunbar are unwilling to acknowledge the realities of the past. And in the absence of that acknowledgement, secrets, old resentments and repressions start to fester. As Bea tells us: 'It's the secrecy keeping this going ... Lies encase the heart, like oysters growing on top of each other. Hard, calcified' (1998:66). Bea carries the stigma of association with her father who, years before, was involved in a boating accident in which both he and a number of the town's children were drowned. This tragedy is seen in an inchoate way as Bea's family's fault. The town's inability to deal with the trauma of this event means that Bea finds it impossible to establish a memorial in the town. The town's choosing not to remember is seen as a sign of its inability to face up to the truth. A memorial can be, as Bea suggests, 'somewhere to reflect' (1998:7), but this is precisely what the people of the town studiously avoid.

Thomson's country town is a place with a pervasive sense of loss and a quiet despair. Death has touched many of Dunbar's families, but the grieving is seen to be a dangerous emotion, too close to madness. Dick and Pam Shaw who run the local drapery are mourning the untimely death of their son Andy who died of a heart attack at the age of 34. Pam is preoccupied with the business of 'just getting on with things': 'onwards and upwards, Dick, let's not dwell' is her mantra to her grieving husband (1998:15). There is something misguided, Thomson suggests, about the insistence on pushing away the realities and tragedies of the past. This is a country town in which the past cannot be acknowledged for fear that it will unravel the delicate balance of the present. The unacknowledged past also provides a powerful context for suspicion and blame to flourish. As Dick points out: 'people say things twice these days and that means they're set in stone' (1998:37). But this is more than the poison of small town gossip, the town folk seem desperate to point the accusatory finger; first identifying Bea as an outsider, and then subjecting her to a campaign of humiliation for crimes that are not all apparent. It does not seem to matter that Bea's 'crimes' are unspecified, it is the fact that scapegoating her provides a release to this community which will go to any lengths to avoid self reflection which might in turn lead to self awareness.

In *Falling Petals*, we witness the contagion of illness as a metaphor for moral decay. In *Navigating* the contagion is pragmatism, the belief that the ends justify the means. Progress is an unassailable 'good', and to stand in its way is simply inexplicable. With Dunbar standing to make tremendous gains from this deal, Bea's objections are brushed aside by Ian's insistence on the need to grasp the 'realities' of the competitive marketplace: 'Thirty-five other shires made submissions to get a prison. Here we are, a breath away' (1998:25). In the same vein and using similar rhetoric, Ian coerces Brent, who runs the local newspaper. Bea has handed the damaging evidence of corruption over to Brent urging him to print an exposé. But Ian is determined to put a stop to this, and he gives Brent some (rather menacing) advice about the new competitive world they find themselves in: 'Brent, if I owned a shitty little throw-away country newspaper ... to take advantage of the Shire's sudden spring into the twenty-first century ... I'd be thinking of being diplomatic, circumspect, and looking at the first edition of real estate in colour' ... (1998:58). The emphasis is on pragmatism, toeing the line, going with the flow, the impossibility of being anti-progress, and then the final direct appeal to self interest. You too will be the beneficiary of the brave new commercial realities – even if it means selling your professional and personal ethics down the river.

Another feature of Thomson's portrait of country town life is the fear and loathing associated with anyone who makes a fuss. It is a part of Bea's downfall that she insists on sticking her neck out. The people of Dunbar demonstrate a tremendous dislike for those who buck the system, or who draw attention to themselves – and Bea makes the mistake of doing precisely this. It is on these grounds that the people of

Dunbar are able to rationalise their humiliation of Bea – believing that she is mad, even dangerous. In small communities, Thomson seems to be arguing, there is a social prohibition on independent thought; eccentricity and boldness are viewed with suspicion, and conformism is an intrinsic good.

The *Australian*'s theatre reviewer McCallum identified the play's skill in its portrayal of the characters of Dunbar, noting in particular that it is the evocation of their emotional lives that gives the play its punch (McCallum 1998). McCallum does not see the play as operating beyond the realm of 'a conventional story of ... individual lives and emotions', commenting that 'the plot is personal rather than political' (McCallum 1998). Kelly, on the other hand, also reviewing for the *Australian*, considers the play's metaphoric and political power. Her review begins: 'Will flagship Australia heed the warnings of those obsessional few who dare to appeal to that democratic accountability we overtly uphold?' (Kelly 1997). Kelly's review of the play acknowledges its contemporary political focus when she argues that: 'Thomson shows herself the foremost analyst of the 1990s malaise, revealing the moral costs as ex-working communities endeavour to assimilate the social and psychological impact of structural unemployment dressed up in buzz words such as "opportunity" or "enterprise"' (Kelly 1997). Kelly sees the broader ideological canvas within which the play is operating when she notes that its exploration of contemporary Australian public values works to 'indict[e] the supine complicity of the many and the visionless rapacity of the few' (Kelly 1997).

As Kelly identifies, Thomson has trained a critical gaze on an 'ordinary' Australian country town and provides insights into the ideas which have informed the state of the nation over the past decade. There is here the pragmatic view that economic reform and progress provide unending opportunities for growth and wealth creation. Ian tells us: 'Christ, the opportunities, you can taste them' (1998:68). That the potential for unfettered economic growth will have its beneficiaries is not being tested here, but, Thomson asks, how might we count the costs? How good is it for the nation? As the play exemplifies, there are moral and social costs in an environment where the market is allowed to determine value. Many of the features of the Australian Legend are deconstructed: rather than manifesting courage, these 'ordinary' Australians are fearful. Not only are they *not* self-reliant, they use blame as a strategy for coping in the world. This rural setting is the locus, not for national pride, but for spiralling moral corruption and greed. Like Rayson and Ellis, Thomson re-reads national myths and discourses in order to establish a complex and reflexive understanding of the nexus between politics, national identity and real life experience.

Last Cab to Darwin

This play by Reg Cribb was written in 2003 (the same year as *Inheritance* and *Falling Petals*). Directed by Jeremy Sims and produced by Sims' Pork Chop Productions, it premiered at the Black Swan Theatre in Perth, before a second season at the Sydney Opera House, and then a regional tour around Australia in 2004. Cribb's work is shaped by his rural origins: 'I'm a country boy; I've got one foot in the country and one in the city. I was schooled in the city but I was brought up in the wheat belt in WA' (Cribb 2005). The intense connection to the country, and his sense of a divide between the urban and rural sectors, is an important motivating factor for him:

> One of the reasons I wanted to write *Last Cab to Darwin* was I imagined all these North Shore people sitting there in the Opera House never having thought about these people in the middle of the outback, never having thought about these godforsaken areas ... and watching it [and] thinking about what this country is about ... I think about this country every single day, isn't that what we're supposed to do? I can't see how we can't not think about the country ... But people are retreating from it. In the 60s people were putting the protests song out there, they were putting the plays out there ... But we're retreating; we switch on *Backyard Blitz* ... (Cribb 2005)

Last Cab to Darwin (2003) is emblematic of Cribb's concern to 'think' about the country. Unlike the other plays in this chapter it has a peripatetic protagonist (Max), and it is through his journey from Broken Hill to Darwin and back again that we come to see Cribb's vision of the Australian countryside. Cribb views the geographic divide between urban and rural Australia as a critical national political issue. Thus Cribb, perhaps more than the other writers discussed here, evokes distance or remoteness as the key signifier of life in rural Australia. Cribb's characters feel themselves to be isolated and removed from everything else. And this isolation produces a sense of melancholy which seeps into every corner of their lives.

Last Cab to Darwin tells the story of Max, a 65-year-old cab driver who has spent all his life in Broken Hill. Max has lived an unadventurous life; he has never married, and is 'as poor as a blackfella' (2003:30). He has spent his adult life driving cabs around the confines of the town – a place described as 'a faded old heap of dust'. There are twenty-seven pubs in Broken Hill, and one of them, the Federal, is where Max meets his mates each night for a drink. When the play opens Max discovers he has stomach cancer and has approximately six months to live. He makes a bold decision: he wants to die by euthanasia; to take control of the process of dying. He sees euthanasia as 'deliverance' from 'being scared' (2003:28). Max finds out that the Northern Territory has passed a 'right to die' bill through parliament, and there is a doctor in Darwin who is a public advocate for, and practitioner of, euthanasia. He decides, despite the protests of his mates, that he will drive his old cab the 3000 kilometres to Darwin in order to receive the deliverance he desires. However, just when Max is at the point of getting his lethal injection, there is a court challenge to the Northern Territory Euthanasia Bill, and the doctor is legally prevented from treating him. Crippled with pain, and against the advice of the doctor, Max gets back in his cab and starts to head back to Broken Hill. He dies on the side of the road.

The play has a three-act structure and moves through a chronological sequence of scenes which help to evoke the sense of a journey. Act 1 of the play takes place in Broken Hill and sets up the premise of the story. As a setting, Cribb portrays the town as a faded, melancholic place where people live with a tangible sense of their own obsolescence. In describing Broken Hill and its environs, the author gives his protagonist a monologue which is striking for its repetition of the words 'nothing' and 'nowhere':

> You can drive down any street here and they all lead to the same place. Nowhere. Then beyond that is the back of nowhere. You don't wanna drive beyond the back of nowhere 'cause you come

> back mad … Why would ya go out there? Why would ya bother?
> As far as the eye can see, there's nothin' … All nothin' does is
> create more nothin'. It's a feedin' frenzy of nothin' out there.
> There's a part of me that loves nothin' 'cause it doesn't have to
> pretend to be anything else but … nothin' (2003:35).

The sense of a philosophical emptiness is a powerful signifier in this play
for the remoteness and marginality of rural Australia. The repetition
of 'nothing' and 'nowhere' emphasises an existential reading of the
landscape; if one lives 'nowhere' surrounded by 'nothing', one is leading
an empty and pointless existence. At the same time, the play is explicitly
not nihilistic. Unlike Ellis' *Falling Petals* which takes the bleakest of
outlooks on life in a country town, this play demonstrates a fondness
for many of the places and people it portrays. This fondness expresses
itself through the play's sense of humour; many of the characters are
fine story-tellers, jokers, and philosophers with a droll take on life. But
this comic element is underscored by a darker existential reading of
the 'realities' of rural life which sees it as a diminished and diminishing
part of Australia. As one of the characters tells us:

> I have nightmares about Sydney and Melbourne … They're
> just perched on the edge of this country and nearly everyone
> lives there. And if they don't live there already, then they want
> to. One day we'll all live there. It's obscene. The sheer weight
> of them will tip this country over. Upend us all and send us
> hurtling into the ocean (2003:49).

The overwhelming cultural force in the nation is urban. That is where
life is, and that leaves the entire rural sector with nothing and nowhere;
this is the play's contention which Cribb realises through this play's
representation of a character's epic (though ultimately pointless)
journey across Australia's dry heartland to take his own life.

In many respects the play's dialogue and comic tone is reminiscent
of the 'ocker' comedies of the 1970s and 1980s. There is a stream
of references to drinking, vomiting and urinating – all the familiar
rhetorical flourishes of the 'ocker' genre. Max's mate Doug likes to
drink and he's been thrown out of most of the pubs in town, including
the Workers Club where he was banned because he 'spewed in the
two-up ring on Anzac Day' (2003:22). There is here a conscious
evocation of explicitly 'Australian' motifs; mateship, disrespect for

protocol, drunkenness, vomiting, Anzac Day and gambling – a grab bag of familiar connotations expressed in a language that is immediately recognisable and distinctive for its earthy comedic qualities.

However, despite the robust comedy of the language, there is also a strong element of the melancholic in this play; people and places alike are on the verge of dying out, and the language of the play reflects something of this dark undertone. In justifying his decision to take his own life, Max tells his friend Polly:

> Do you wanna watch me fade away ... like old Mr Fester? ... By the end there, he was lookin' worse than the carcass of my old ute that I left on the side of the road out past Silverton. By the end there, he'd look at you with eyes that said: 'Kill me or don't fuckin' talk to me' (2003:31).

The language here, and throughout the play, reveals a dark, gallows humour reminiscent in some respects of the cemetery scene in Rayson's *Inheritance* where the characters tell inappropriate jokes about penises at a family funeral. In Cribb's play there is also an intermingling of 'ocker' comedy with stories of death and dying. The notion of near death is one that the play reiterates. Not only is the protagonist dying, but so is the environment. The play portrays a number of different rural communities all of which have one thing in common – they are in a terminal state of decay. Max has a bleak prognosis:

> This country? I love it to death but ... it's hurting. It doesn't think much of itself and it's not happy. It doesn't know what it wants to be, doesn't know where it's going and has no bloody idea how to make itself happy. It's a rotting carcass. Everything that it thought it ever was is disappearing before its eyes (2003:75).

Cribb portrays a world of townships which are barren places with an air of desperation about them. Recalling Max's earlier monologue emphasising the 'nothingness' which defines life in Broken Hill, Ted Mingle, Mayor of Todmorden, describes the way the town has been gradually stripped of all its basic services: 'How much have we left in this town? Nothing ... No banks, no high school, no doctor, no hospital, no dentist, no hairdresser, no footy club, no kindergarten ... nothing. Sweet bugger all!' (2003:49). It is a picture of a community brought to its knees – a phenomenon which all the writers here have explored in one way or another. And the people who inhabit the places Max visits on his road trip are, like Max himself, fading into death and obscurity.

In Act 2 Max is on the road and we meet a range of characters, living in remote locations, as he travels up to Darwin. The further he travels, the more it seems that coming from Broken Hill (ironically) makes Max a 'Big city fella' (2003:39). Inside a shop, somewhere south of Maree, Max finds Dot, Ces and Bob who are glued to the television watching the midday movie, swatting flies and drinking beer. They are unforthcoming with Max, suspicious of him in a way that tells us they are wary of outsiders. At this point the play takes something of an Absurdist turn. The scene plays out a static situation where the dialogue consists of short exchanges between the four characters. Martin Esslin describes the dialogue in *Waiting for Godot* as having: 'the curious repetitive quality of the cross-talk comedians' patter' – and this might also be said of Cribb's writing here (Esslin 1987:47). The familiar taciturnity of the men of the Australian bush is evoked in this scene, but within an Absurdist context, which helps the play continue to build an existential undertow. The absurdist elements of the play give it a different feel to the others discussed here. The style of the work slips between a number of different 'modes': naturalistic elements are inflected with absurdist moments (a song and dance routine in Act 2 where the cast perform the 'Tidy Town Song' is illustrative of this); along with dream-like or surrealistic passages as Max's death draws nearer. Cribb is engaged in a very different project to Ellis who, in *Falling Petals*, provides a disaffected picture of the characters who inhabit his fictional country town. Cribb, on the other hand, demonstrates affection for the characters he portrays. Yet, Cribb does not sentimentalise or heroise them as 'battlers'. Indeed, the idea that these people who 'do it hard' are the famed 'Aussie battlers' is also deconstructed. Max says: 'Farmers, miners, jackeroos ... we used to be called battlers. Now we're called losers'. In the struggle to keep going the 'battlers have all fallen by the wayside. Too bone bloody tired to keep going. Or too drunk' (2003:61).

The reviews of the play draw attention to its Australian subject matter and familiar cultural references. One reviewer describes the play as 'a gutsy Aussie yarn', and another notes the play's strong focus on the portrait of 'weather-beaten' Australian men (Boland 2004a; Young 2004). The reviews also note the general appeal of Cribb's writing. Cribb makes it clear that he wants to make popular theatre which engages with contemporary political issues:

> If you can create something that is going to make people think, make them laugh or make them cry all at once then you are doing your job. You want bums on seats. Every playwright wants bums on seats. There is no point being an angry old bolshie if people are going to run away screaming. Find a way to cloak that political message in something a bit more entertaining ... I really believe in entertaining theatre but I believe in entertaining theatre with a message (Cribb 2005).

This interest in capturing a broad audience and using the theatre to communicate political concerns shows that Cribb is cognisant of the commercial realities which have come to circumscribe much of contemporary mainstream theatre. But Cribb qualifies this by adding that he wanted to 'drag people into the theatre who never go':

> When *The Return* was on in Perth there were a couple of bikies sitting in the audience because they had heard there were a couple of rough nuts in it – and I went, "my job is done". I felt very happy about that. That's all I wanted to see. They would never [otherwise] come to the theatre, sitting there amongst all these middle-class people. [And] farmers came to see *Last Cab to Darwin*. My job is done (Cribb 2005).

Like Rayson, Ellis and Thomson, Cribb has used the setting of the country town to stage a two-fold investigation in this play. On the one hand this drama looks at the diminished state of the rural sector and asks some existential questions about its chances of survival. Max's illness makes a well-matched metaphor for the state of the country town. On the other hand, Cribb is also investigating the state of the nation; using a familiar iconography, idiom and sense of humour, Cribb takes a critical rather than celebratory look at the value of the nationalist discourses of the fair go in an environment where only those on one side of the geographic divide are the beneficiaries.

Between them these plays were performed for audiences in Victoria, NSW, Queensland and Western Australia, and *Last Cab to Darwin* also toured to Tasmania, the Northern Territory and South Australia. Thus, their public and political significance as dramatic mainstream works is underwritten by their *national* address. Despite their differences, these plays share an engagement in the task of raising public debate about the state of the nation. In his discussion of the role of the public intellectual, Furedi notes that they 'often raise disturbing questions about prevailing customs and assumptions'; they are concerned with 'social engagement' and their objective is to 'influence society' (Furedi 2004:34–5). These qualities are apparent in the work investigated here and this is evidenced in many of the critical responses to the plays which do not simply account for the works' dramatic achievements but explicitly comment on their value as social and political commentary. Thus the reviews of these plays emphasise 'relevance' and topicality and the political consequences of addressing multiple and 'competing' audiences (Ball 2003; Herbert 2003a). The reviews also note that the stand-out quality of such trenchant political drama is that it can be 'unsettling' and make audiences 'uncomfortable' (On 2003a; Kelly 1997). Arguably, then the intellectual objective of these writers, to stir up public debate, is indeed being realised as the critics note the audience's confrontation with important issues in the public domain.

The plays discussed in this chapter are presented as open to literal and metaphoric readings of their subject matter. In literal terms, they share an interest in interrogating economic rationalism and the way in which large-scale economic reforms of the 1990s left rural Australia in a state of degradation. The rise of Hanson's One Nation, and the geographic inequalities to which it responded, provides the political context for this work and the plays address the political and economic processes by which that marginalisation occurred. This attempt to grapple with real world issues and to create dramas which speak to people's experiences of profound economic change lends them a political edge. They engage with the politics of the day and the realities of rural life in order to provoke and challenge urban audiences.

At the same time, they operate at a metaphoric level. In contrast to the film *Sunday Too Far Away*, all the plays discussed in this chapter provide reinterpretations of Ward's bush legend; here the myth (exemplified in the film) has been politicised. The country town acts as a metaphor for the nation, and a locus for a critical approach to nationalist rhetoric. Hanson's political success was, in part, a function of her capacity to promulgate essentialist discourses about Australian-ness – discourses which spoke to many in the marginalised rural sector. Similarly the rhetoric of the Howard government references the 'Australian way' and 'Australian values' to claim the Australian legend in order to 'fill out ... the picture of the consensual mainstream of Australian life' (Brett 2003:204). The writers discussed here contest this ongoing national-cultural project. They deconstruct the unifying myth-making that has in the past seen rural Australia as a place for defining a unique Australian identity. By their interrogation of the potency of conventional national symbols and rhetoric, they demonstrate their markedly critical nationalism.

Simon Gleeson as Jess and Melissa Jaffer as Vi in the 2004 Sydney Theatre Company production of *Harbour*. (Photo: Heidrun Löhr)

CHAPTER 4

GLOBALISATION & CLASS

The English playwright Harold Pinter has outlined the particular problems that political theatre presents for the writer: 'Sermonising has to be avoided at all costs', he observes. 'The characters must be allowed to breathe their own air. The author cannot confine or constrict them to satisfy his own taste or disposition or prejudice' (Pinter 2005). The writers discussed in this chapter can be distinguished from many other mainstream playwrights by their clear interest in writing about the political issues of the day and in challenging the powers of Australian institutions within the national and political spheres – governments, corporations, universities, business and the press. But they are also united by the concern, identified by Pinter, to create theatre which avoids didacticism.

The idea that the arts are good for social health and well being emerges from the instrumentalist thinking around the arts. In this view, the writer is a teacher or instructor, and the theatre a place where the audience will be 'schooled'. It is a view that is nicely encapsulated in the expression 'cultural spinach', art that is unpalatable but good for you (Jensen 2003). A key issue for playwrights is to grapple with political subject matters without cooking up cultural spinach. They must, therefore, develop dramaturgical strategies which allow them to explore the political terrain without resorting to didacticism. In doing so they portray politics as a complex set of economic, social and ideological tensions in which difficult and sometimes contradictory beliefs and values come into play. Indeed, contradiction is an important device – contradictions and tensions designed to make audiences feel that they must make up their own minds.

There are theatre artists and commentators who argue that this kind of theatre writing is indeed instrumentalist; plays become catalogues of contemporary social issues, so the argument goes, all rendered 'safe' for ready consumption by the writer's middle-class reformist intentions and conservative techniques. Schlusser, for example, takes Australian theatre to task for being generally dominated by a theatre practice which is really 'staged literature … [that] includes some Shavian social do-goodery' (2005). But, as Kershaw points out, attitude is a relative matter: what for some is didactic and reactionary, for others it is provocative and contemporary. So instead of attempting to make categorical judgements about the political effectiveness of their work, it is interesting to consider how the creators of the work themselves understand the nature of their task.

Glenn D'Cruz in his analysis of the Melbourne Workers Theatre production *Who's Afraid of the Working Class?* (2000) argues that the play makes a legitimate claim to the genre of political theatre because it demonstrates: 'a sophisticated understanding of the complexities of contemporary mechanisms of social and political stratification' (2005:210). For D'Cruz, the sophistication of the political analysis underpinning the drama makes it significant. Theatre work of this nature, D'Cruz argues, 'reminds us that "political theatre", however unfashionable the term might be, is not a spent force' (2005:217). The plays discussed here reinforce D'Cruz's argument and suggest that the impulse to write drama informed by a sophisticated reading of the political terrain is alive and well in the contemporary Australian theatre scene. The nature of this political engagement requires an understanding, in broad terms, of some of the history of political theatre writing in Australia.

Australian Political Theatre: Brief Background

Louis Esson, writing in the early twentieth century, was a seminal figure in the development of a consciously nationalist Australian theatre practice informed by socialist sympathies (Fitzpatrick 1995). Esson founded the Pioneer Players, dedicated to the establishment of a nationalist folk drama in which the mythic figure of the bushman-hero was the 'central symbol' (1995:182). Inspired by the Abbey Theatre in Dublin, the Pioneer Players was committed to the production of

Australian plays and provided a showcase for Esson's work including *The Drovers* (1923) and *The Bride of Gospel Place* (1926).

Subsequently, the task of producing a radicalised theatre practice in Australia came to define the work of the New Theatre movement, begun in 1932 in most Australian capital cities as part of a loosely affiliated network of international workers' theatres. A key figure in the Melbourne New Theatre group was Esson's wife, Hilda Esson, who looked to the New Theatre to deliver 'the sort of revolutionary art' which she felt had not been realised in the work of the Pioneer Players (Fitzpatrick 1995:298). O'Brien notes that much of the work of the New Theatre was 'unashamedly didactic' in its attack on capitalism and its support for the Soviet way of life (1995). Along with pioneering productions of plays by Brecht, the New Theatre produced Clifford Odet's call for strike action, *Waiting for Lefty*, in 1936 (Milne 2004:78). For three decades the New Theatre provided a training ground for Australian theatre practitioners concerned with social and political critique: notably the playwright Mona Brand who produced, between 1953 and 1976, a steady stream of satirical reviews and political plays; along with Betty Roland (*War on the Waterfront* produced in 1939); Oriel Gray (*Let's be Offensive* produced in 1943); Dymphna Cusack (*Pacific Paradise* produced in 1955); and Dick Diamond whose popular folk musical *Reedy River* (1953) dominated the New Theatre's repertoire in the mid-1950s (O'Brien 1995). Harper maintains that the New Theatre's production and promotion of Australian work, and its use of popular theatre forms, was a significant legacy for Australian political theatre. (Harper 1984:71).

Certainly both the Pioneer Players and the New Theatre helped to inform later theatre practices. McCallum notes that the period of intensely nationalistic theatre at the APG in the late 1960s and early 1970s took up the nationalist project and the various tropes exemplified in the works of Esson and others of his contemporaries such as Katharine Susannah Prichard (McCallum 1995). The notion of a politicised theatre practice using popular theatre forms such as vaudeville and street theatre informed the APG's work from its inception in the late 1960s and it was not the only New Wave theatre to rediscover agitprop. Meyrick argues that the political force of New

Wave theatre was shaped by its commitment to producing work through which 'society could see itself on stage': theatre was a political project, no longer 'peripheral or ornamental', but fundamental to the way society understood itself (Meyrick 2002:64). There was a concern, too, to build a recognisably Australian voice; the APG, for instance, sought to create a political theatre, informed by the radical traditions of European theatre practices, which addressed itself to the 'new nationalist' ethos encouraged by the Whitlam government and the newly established mechanisms for supporting Australian arts and culture through the Australia Council. The nationalist project which had defined so much of the history of political theat^ ' in Australia, from the Pioneer Players and the New Theatre movement through to the New Wave, was engaged in the task of broadcasting a radical nationalist vision.

Fotheringham observes that one of the chief legacies of the APG was the way many of its practitioners sought to 'institutionalise alternative and ... overtly political theatre practices' through what he calls 'narrowcasting' – that is, to produce work for specific audiences (Fotheringham 1992:74). This task of targeting specific audiences informed much of the post-New Wave political theatre from the late 1970s and through the 1980s which saw its objective as addressing specific 'geographical, ethnic, gender, class, lifestyle and special interest groups' (Fotheringham 1992:76). Indeed the period saw a tendency to define 'political' theatre in terms of the audience to which it was directed such that the choice of audience became 'the major political statement by which [to] challenge the present construction of the Australian *polis*, particularly in its continuing adherence to a middle-class and middle-aged male Anglo-Celtic hierarchy ...' (Fotheringham 1992:76).

Two forms of political theatre in particular came to prominence: feminist theatre and community theatre, and both were important in shaping contemporary practices. Informed by feminist theory, feminist theatre sought to 'abandon the hierarchical organising principles of traditional form that served to elide women from discourse' (Case 1988:129). The contribution of feminist theatre to contemporary political theatre writing is significant. Certainly, playwrights such as

Hannie Rayson, Katherine Thomson and Patricia Cornelius (if not all of the women writers of the current era) could be seen to be the beneficiaries of the pioneering efforts of the women's theatre groups of the 1970 and 1980s and playwrights such as Dorothy Hewett, who effectively paved the way for subsequent generations of female theatre artists to come to prominence. Hewett was prolific in the 1980s with many produced scripts and a national profile for her plays which 'put sex and desire on stage in ways that had not been seen' (Moore 2002).

Rayson's plays in the 1980s took a gendered approach to the analysis of Australian society, and she explains how feminism was important in shaping the focus of her playwriting at that time:

> Feminism would have to be the key politicising influence ... I know that's what shaped my politics and ... the approach to the work, to the subject matter. I was fuelled by a desire to put women on the stage and to give women a voice ... And I wanted to drive the narrative with female concerns and female protagonists. And also the subject matter was often about the difficulties between the sexes – a subject that I have very little interest in now (Rayson 2005a).

While Rayson no longer sees gender as the primary framework for her writing, she acknowledges the importance of feminism and its focus on the nature and distribution of social power in shaping her interest in political theatre. Thus for example, while the lesson from 1980s feminism – that the personal is political – still resonates with Rayson she now adds a caveat:

> I do think the personal is political, but I also think that there are great public debates that are not personal that one needs to tackle ... who exercises power is something that crosses from the public to the private and back again all the time, and that's the kind of stuff I'm really interested in (Rayson 2005a).

Katherine Thomson shares this interest in the intersection of the public and the private. Like Rayson, Thomson, was influenced by the community theatre and feminist theatre movements of the 1980s and feels herself to have benefited from women's theatre. Indeed, the support she received from the 1982 Women and Arts Festival to write her first play *A Change in the Weather* (1982) was both financial and moral:

> I got $2000 [to cover the cost of] the writer, director, two actors and [the] entire production. But the fact that the committee felt my proposal [was] worthy of support was a wonderful boost. Being under the umbrella of this festival [also] gave me some confidence that I must be doing something right ... The connections I made in that time have enriched my life (Thomson 2005a).

The legacy of this period is manifested in Thomson's belief in the capacity of theatre to inspire change. When asked to comment on the political purpose of her work, Thomson comments: 'I always paraphrase [James Elroy] Flecker "the purpose of theatre is not to change men's souls but make them glad they have one"' (Thomson 2005a). For Thomson (like Rayson) the enmeshing of the personal with the political, a product of the 1980s feminist movement, remains a powerful influence. This is demonstrated in her plays discussed here: *Navigating* (1997), *Wonderlands* (2003) and *Harbour* (2004) – all of which use community-based research, and seek to explore the notion of politics as lived experience. These plays maintain a sharp awareness of regional specificities and the drama (and the politics) flows from this context. Thomson's interest in the struggles of working-class life, apparent from her first play, continues to define the rest of her oeuvre.

Another persistent feature of feminist theatre has been its commitment to deconstructing the myths of Australian national identity and its assertion that 'gender is as central as race to the Australian imaginary' (Gilbert 1998:145). Helen Thomson (1998) has also argued that one of the telling features of feminist theatre practices in Australia (distinguishing it from similar work in the US and UK) is that it has made a 'deliberate contribution' to the ongoing discussion of national identity in the theatre. This task of identifying and deconstructing hegemonic practices and values is, arguably, the significant political legacy of feminist theatre for all the writers considered in this book.

In a similar vein the legacies of the community theatre movement in Australia, from the mid-1970s to the 1980s are important in the genesis of political theatre writing for some of the writers considered here. Community theatre developed as a part of a larger community arts movement which emphasised the idea of 'artworkers' producing work in and for specific communities. Thus, instead of seeing the value of the individual artist only within the commercial marketplace, the community theatre movement was defined by a democratic ethos that privileged audience access and participation over the notions of elitism and excellence traditionally associated with the 'high arts' (Kirby 1991). It rejected the notion of 'high arts' and the audience as consumer and instead was committed to working within 'cultures of marginalised, suppressed and oppressed social groups ... alienated from the processes of decision-making within the society' (Watt and Pitts 1991:122).

From the late 1980s and through the 1990s political theatre has continued to be in evidence at the Melbourne Workers Theatre and Sidetrack Theatre in Sydney. Sidetrack Theatre (now Sidetrack Performance Group) emerged out of the community theatre movement and was originally committed to touring its productions to workplaces and community-based venues in working-class areas of Sydney. The early work of the company explored the multicultural and immigrant experiences of the local inner-city community.

Melbourne Workers Theatre, which began life in 1987 supported through the Australia Council's Art and Working Life Program, is a company dedicated to making theatre for, with and about working-class people, and it undertakes this work, as D'Cruz points out, in a political and cultural context which 'displaces class as a primary category of identity' (D'Cruz 2005:207). Playwright Andrew Bovell started writing for the Melbourne Workers Theatre in 1987 after graduating from the VCA Writers' course. He explains:

> It was a very influential period in my thinking about what theatre needed to do and what it could do. Melbourne Workers Theatre was essentially a socialist theatre company, the theatre was ... performing a larger function, a function beyond itself, it was a tool for change ... we believed passionately in the mid-1980s that by telling people stories of a particular kind, you recognised and you empowered those people. So, as a writer [I] made a

conscious choice not to write stories of the middle class but to
write from a working-class [perspective] (Bovell 2002a).

The commitment was twofold: to produce an explicitly political theatre;
and to situate and develop it for workers (often in their workplaces),
using their stories and experiences as the basis for the drama. Bovell's
plays for the Melbourne Workers Theatre included *State of Defence*
(1987) and *The Ballad of Lois Ryan* (1988).

The Melbourne Workers Theatre remains committed, as D'Cruz
puts it, 'to keeping the heritage of class struggle in play' (2005:207).
To that end the company has foregrounded the work of other explicitly
political playwrights concerned with the portrayal of class struggle
– notably Patricia Cornelius whose plays, produced by Melbourne
Workers Theatre, include *Dusting Our Knees* (1988) and *Daily Grind*
(1992) co-written with Vicki Reynolds. Cornelius, who comes from a
working-class background, describes her political education as having
been informed by both feminism and Marxism, and most particularly
by the insights that came from class analysis:

> ... the notions of class absolutely made sense to me. I also think
> in some ways as an artist it liberates you. If you come from
> trash like I do, then the voice that you have is a terribly under-
> confident or unsteady one, because you're always afraid that
> someone is going to realise you're from trash; you've got nothing
> fucking to say baby, you don't know nothing. So you kind of
> hide that. It's as if you've got no right to the arts in that way. But
> then with writing, to find that voice, I know that voice ... That's
> the world I wanted to write for (Cornelius 2002).

Another theatre practitioner of note is Scott Rankin, artistic director of
the national youth arts project Big hART whose large-scale community
projects encourage community participation and addresses topical
political issues such as homeless youth (*kNOT@Home* 2002–2004)
and public housing (*Northcott Narratives* 2002–2007): his work is
underpinned by a commitment to performing in non-traditional spaces
and collaborating with community participants.

Rankin's work and that of the Melbourne Workers Theatre are
good examples of the ongoing legacies of the community theatre
movement. The political analysis of power relations which lies at the

heart of community theatre, its democratic impulse, and its concern to represent or address the voices of people outside the dominant culture have resonance for the contemporary political theatre writing discussed here.

For Bovell, the community arts movement not only shaped his interest in political subject matters, it also suggested to him new collaborative methods for creating the work:

> ... the way we made work, which ... remained very strong with me ... You don't privilege the authorial voice; you privilege the content, the subject. It is not about the playwright, it's about collaboration between a number of theatre workers. We called ourselves theatre workers or theatre practitioners, not writers or directors (Bovell 2002a).

In explaining the legacies of this period, Bovell explains:

> I can only do what I continue to do which is [to] take a critical position in regard to my own culture. I don't subscribe to anything so high falutin' as to suggest that this is a noble function. [But] it is an important one (Bovell 2002a).

This is not to say that community theatre is the sole antecedent of the political plays that are the focus of this book. Indeed, none of the writers interviewed described themselves or their role as 'artworkers' within communities. In recent times the term community arts itself has largely been made redundant as the philosophies and activities associated with it are integrated into a larger category of cultural development policies linking arts and culture to urban planning and social welfare (Hawkes 2001). Nevertheless for writers such as Bovell, Rayson, Thomson and Cribb, the principle of making theatre which gives a voice and debates issues related to those outside of hegemonic political processes remains a compelling and primary motivating factor in their writing. At the same time, these writers are, like those of previous generations, putting a politicised discussion of nationhood at the centre of their dramatic practices.

One of the most significant producers of political theatre is playwright Daniel Keene. In the 1990s Keene teamed up with the director and designer Ariette Taylor to form the Keene/Taylor Theatre Project. They achieved considerable critical acclaim for the production of a substantial body of work (more than twenty short plays) between 1997 and 2002. Keene's play *Scissors, Paper, Rock* (first performed in 1998 and again in 2002) is 'the tragedy of a working-class man in a world where the working class no longer exists' (Keene/Taylor Project 2002). Despite the class-based framework for the drama, it elides polemic and uses a style that is minimalist and ironic. In 21 short scenes, the play focuses on the lives and experiences of working-class men and women. This is a matter of ongoing interest for Keene, a commitment that stems from the belief, not that 'theatre can change anything', but that it 'has the possibility, if not the obligation, to be of its time. We live in a difficult time' (Keene/Taylor Project 2002). In defining the difficulty of the time, Keene says: 'It seems to me that at present the powerful have very little to teach us, except how to cope with their failures and crimes, and absolutely nothing to teach the future' (Keene 2006). To this end, Keene's plays focus not on the powerful but on the powerless, those on the edges of society – those who 'cannot confer nor confirm power' (Keene 2006).

Keene's plays belong to a modernist European tradition and, rather than focusing on the specificities of Australian political experience, are addressed to the politics of a globalised, post-national world: a theatre practice which he describes as 'a place without borders' (Keene 2006). Keene explains:

> A theatre, for me, is a kind of common, an open space, a town square, circle of stones. Here is where we gather, to discuss the day's news, to share our gossip, to hatch our plots, to lament, to celebrate, to be idle, to display ourselves, to remember, to dream and to demand; an empty space that offers a freedom available to all (Keene 2006)

It is interesting to note that in comparison to the other writers discussed here, Keene has little mainstream profile, but he enjoys the highest international profile with his plays being regularly produced in Europe, especially in France.

Michael Gurr is a Melbourne-based playwright whose plays reveal a persistent interest in Australian politics. Gurr was taken up as a young playwright by the MTC's literary manager, Ray Lawler, who took responsibility for seeing that the MTC also encouraged emerging local talent (Gurr 2002). As MTC's Playwright in Residence from 1982, Gurr had a number of plays produced at the MTC including *Magnetic North* (1982). Establishing a creative partnership with the director Bruce Myles, Gurr went on to have a long association with the Playbox Theatre which, throughout the 1990s, produced a series of his plays including *Sex Diary of an Infidel* (1992), *Underwear, Perfume & Crash Helmet* (1994), *Jerusalem* (1996) and *Crazy Brave* (2000). In addition to working as a playwright, Gurr was also a speechwriter for the then Victorian Labor Opposition Leader, Steve Bracks in the campaign that (unexpectedly) returned the ALP to power in 1999. This close alignment of theatre writing with an active political engagement is evident in many of Gurr's plays.

Jerusalem, according to its playwright, is 'a play without a villain' (Gurr 2006:251). It tells the story of two sets of socially concerned idealists: one is a small group of men and women who belong to a Christian volunteer prison visiting service; and the other a group of Labor Party members. Each group wants to do 'good' works and each person is motivated by a strong sense of social and political responsibility. At the same time they are flawed characters; none of them are heroic, some of them are deeply irritating, and each of them struggles to make any difference to other people's lives. Indeed, their good works, this 'mopping up after people who've fallen in a heap' largely goes unnoticed (Gurr 1996:40). But despite the play's questioning of the effectiveness of 'goodness', the pointlessness of trying to improve things, it nonetheless sees value in leading a moral life. Gurr might have equally said that this was a play without heroes, but we admire the struggle to maintain a sense of idealism in the face of weakness and misery.

Crazy Brave is also interested in the issue of idealism. It contrasts the burnt out cynicism of Harold, an old left-wing lawyer and icon of the Labor movement, with the determined idealism of a group of young urban activists who are fed up with mainstream politics. Australia, they argue, is a 'nation of sleepwalkers' and the population will not be awakened by reasonable argument, but only by acts of civil disruption to produce an 'eruption of chaos' (Gurr 2000:25). Gurr paints a picture of Australia as suffering from crippling political enervation. Radical political change is unlikely: generations of young Australians may wish to fight the good fight but inevitably 'go down ... to the chloroform of sunlight' (Gurr 2000:43).

Gurr is not the only playwright to have noted a diminishing idealism in Australia and been interested in tracing the impact of the political and economic agenda of the Australian Right. A number of plays look at the ways in which economic rationalism affects the lives of working people. They seek to contribute to public debate about the values which should underpin our political and social lives, and in so doing they address the diminishing currency of social liberalism in Australia.

Social Liberalism

Marian Sawer traces what she sees as the gradual erosion of social liberalism in Australia and the various economic policies such as wage arbitration, family endowments and aged pensions which underpinned it. Social liberalism, she argues, had provided the philosophical basis for the ethical operations of the state with its emphasis on the common good and a fair go for all. Since the late nineteenth century social-liberal ideas have been significant factors in shaping Australian political institutions and, in Sawer's terms, the concepts of equal opportunity and social justice are its cornerstones. The social movements of the 1970s and 1980s such as the women's movement, gay and lesbian groups, Indigenous rights groups and immigrants from Non-English-Speaking backgrounds contributed to the development of social liberalism by 'offering new understandings of difference and of how difference must be acknowledged and accommodated' (Sawer 2003:167). However with the rise of neo-liberalism in the 1990s, many of these ideas have been critically reviewed and found wanting; the 'laws of competition' are now seen to be the principal measure by which human affairs are to be governed, with the free market representing the high watermark of social and economic achievement. Indeed as Sawer puts it: 'the idea of the market contract [has become] the epitome of liberty' (2003:9). McKnight suggests that these changes in thinking and their 'deeper assumptions about human nature' constitute a 'modest revolution' in Australia (2005:50). In the light of these 'revolutionary' philosophical shifts, the equality-seeking social movements of the 1970s and

1980s have been subjected to revisionist re-readings. Contemporary campaigners for social justice and equality have become 'special interest groups' or rent-seekers, thus apparently justifying the state's view that 'recognition and accommodation of difference are at the expense of "ordinary" citizens' (Sawer 2003:185). The plays in this chapter explore this changed political environment and its broad philosophical and social ramifications. Each of them, in different ways, is concerned to understand how the promotion of the neo-liberalist idea of 'governing for the mainstream' has discouraged oppositional voices and discourses.

Tearing up the Social Contract

Katherine Thomson's play *Harbour* is a response to the economic and industrial reforms in Australia from the mid-1990s. These reforms, which had begun under the Labor government in the late 1980s, had a profound affect on the way people experienced their working lives. As Michael Pusey points out, these changes, brought about by globalisation, have involved a 'top-down process of structural reform that is aimed at maximizing economic efficiency and productivity' (2003:47). In an effort to maximise productivity, corporations have sought to reduce labour costs, and instituted labour market reforms which have had a significant impact on the 'received understandings of jobs, work and working life' (Pusey 2003:48). In Pusey's view, reforms begun under Labor in the 1990s continue to shape industrial relations policies today, and the result is the 'tearing up of the social contract' that has traditionally defined the nature of working life in Australia. The rush towards a market-oriented society has created a political environment where 'the power of the stronger part is unbridled by collective agreements with the weaker one' (2003:49).

Like Pusey, Sawer sees the development of compulsory conciliation and arbitration as a key feature of Australia's history of industrial relations from the late-nineteenth century. The commitment to compulsory arbitration, initiated by nineteenth-century Australian liberals, has been a cornerstone of social liberalist political philosophy. However, in the late 1990s the government, in partnership with business, sought to break union power. Thomson's play *Harbour* investigates this historical moment as it turns on the relationship between industrial reform and the nature of work. It is a topic that continues to be relevant in the light of recent industrial relations policies which encourage non-unionised labour and individual workplace agreements. *Harbour* offers a portrait of how economic rationalism and globalisation has forced a renegotiation of the social contract between the government and the Australian workforce, a renegotiation that has empowered one group at the expense of the other, leaving a trail of disenfranchised workers in its wake. Thomson's fictional rendering of this phenomenon is supported by Pusey's account of how labour market deregulation, industry restructuring and the weakening of organised labour, particularly since the late 1990s, have produced winners – big business and corporations – and losers – wage and salary earners – in both the public and private spheres.

Harbour

Harbour was produced in 2004 at the Sydney Theatre Company, directed by Robyn Nevin. The play is set in the context of the 1998 dispute between the maritime workers and Patrick Stevedores. The company and the government both accused the waterside workers of corruption and poor work practices and the workforce was sacked. The dispute which followed threatened to overturn the industrial relations arrangements that had previously been in place. The Howard government, which had been in power for two years, had sought to bring about changes in industrial relations law that would seriously threaten the power of Australian unions. The wharves, with their history of unionised labour, were the site of the battle, and it quickly became 'an ideological litmus test' for the government's planned industrial reforms (Manne 2001:25). Thomson describes the starting point for writing this play and insists that she did not begin it with a particular political point-of-view:

> ... you [have to] go into this not necessarily prepared to see what side you are going to fall on ... you had to be prepared to start researching the waterfront dispute and discover that, in fact, Patrick's was right: that the Maritime Union was sending [Patrick's] down the gurgler and I had to say this on my first

day [researching the play] at the Maritime Union – 'look, I'm coming to use your library but there is every possibility that I'll come down on the other side'. They took that risk and I took that risk ... (Thomson 2005a).

Thomson's two-act play focuses on the story of a family which represents a range of sides in the debate: waterside workers (wharfies), union representatives, non-union labour (scabs), business interests and mercenaries. Like much of Thomson's work, this play investigates a family's emotional and personal struggles within the context of a national, political struggle over values. The set of the STC production reinforced this relationship by featuring a large rusted metal backdrop against which all the intimate family scenes were played out. The author describes its effect: 'as if a container vessel had found its way into the living room' (Thomson 2005b:xviii). In the first act Sandy, a wharfie all his working life, has returned home to his estranged wife Vi, and their four children. He has been gone for six years, living on his retrenchment money in Darwin with his girlfriend, but the relationship has finished and Sandy has returned determined to get his family back together. He has cancer and wants to be reconciled with them before he dies. Sandy has the idea that Vi and their four adult children will come with him to the family's dilapidated shack at the beach, and that they would all be together again. However, Sandy discovers that his tough ex-wife, Vi, is in no mood for a reconciliation, and that the members of his family are irrevocably split along ideological lines.

This personal family drama is played out in the context of an escalating war between the government and the waterside workers which comes to a head in Act 2. The stevedoring company, Reynolds, with the support of the government, has hired a group of 76 non-union workers to be trained on the wharves in Dubai with a view to replacing the unionised workforce on the Australian docks. The situation is tense. The wharfies have been accused, by a government determined to break the power of the Australian Maritime Union, of poor work practices and corruption. Matt, Sandy's son, is a union leader who, like his father, is committed to role of the union in protecting workers' rights. But at the same time Matt belongs to a younger generation and he's heard too many stories about the glory days of the union movement. While he is following in his father and grandfather's footsteps, and there is a powerful sense of his political inheritance, Matt wants to make his own way. And it is a critical moment for him as the Reynolds Company makes a move to sack its workforce on the docks. As the union plans industrial action, Matt's job is to 'bring the membership with him'. He is a pragmatist, less driven by ideology than his father, and more compelled by the necessity of winning good wages and conditions for the workers: 'My bigger picture', he explains to his father, 'is that they're all well paid, a bit more flexibility and a bit less Marx ...' (2005b:28).

Where Matt embodies a pragmatic approach to the union and its role, Sandy has a more profound sense of the intrinsic importance of the union movement to the valuing of labour. He carries a strong connection to the history of union struggles embodied in the stories he tells of his own father: 'A man of principles. Lines that were drawn on the ground before he was born and they were not crossed' (2005b:1). For Sandy, the union movement is about the importance of united effort and the capacity for workers to stand together in the face of injustice: ' ... a man on his own is just that, but when people get together ... they can give each other the courage to dance through flames' (2005b:2). But Sandy is, perhaps, one of a dying breed; his ideological certainty is not reflected in the attitudes of the younger generation. Sandy finds that in his absence the world he thought he knew has changed: the union movement is under ferocious attack, and in his private life his children and ex-wife are dealing with their own intense hurts and disappointments.

Sandy's daughter Belle works in Human Resources at the Australian Stock Exchange; she has shaken off any remnant of her working-class union background, and has re-shaped herself to suit the conservative and materialistic ethos of her professional environment. Belle claims that the disappearance of her father was 'the best thing that ever happened. We could forget about happy families and get on with our lives' (2005b:38). But for Belle getting on with her life has involved a complete rejection of her family's politics and a denial of her background. Accosting her at work, her father jokes 'don't let on you come from a wharfie family, they might start blaming you if things get pinched' (2005b:40). Belle defends the actions of the Reynolds Company; she argues that the company is losing money because of low productivity on the docks, and that the looming industrial crisis is due to the unchecked power of the unions. Belle represents the new management ethos which emerged in the late 1990s as a function of economic rationalism. She announces to her family: 'I work for people who think every employee in this town should go to work every day afraid of losing their jobs' (2005b:65). As a statement, this encapsulates the vast divide between the worker-oriented objectives of the union movement, held dear by Sandy, and the new tough rationalism of the corporate sector. As Brett points out, the late 1990s saw the promulgation of management discourses, in both the private and public sphere, which replaced old ideas about 'equity and service' with a new emphasis on 'rewards for quantifiable individual performances' (2002:172).

Vi, Sandy's estranged wife, has been toughened by life. Thomson renders her as an unforgiving and unsentimental character with a laconic sense of humour, a fierce temper and passionate principles. Like the character of Bea in *Navigating* who is driven and often irritating, Vi is another difficult woman. We admire her for her capacity to cope with difficult circumstances, but she is unyielding and she alienates her children with her uncompromising stance and fixed opinions. There is an irony in this portrait: Vi values straight talking above all else, but she is complicit in maintaining, over many years, the deception that Jess is her own son rather than, as it turns out, her grandson. In the same way, Thomson creates a portrait of Sandy so that the audience understands the complex ironies of the interaction of the personal and the public lives of these working-class characters. In his personal life Sandy has acted without principle; he runs off with his girlfriend and his retrenchment money and thereby impoverishes and humiliates his wife and family. At the same time, however, he is passionately committed to the union movement and the principled stance about the rights of a fair go for workers. Unlike Vi, Sandy is also prepared to admit he made a mistake, to acknowledge that his behaviour was weak and self serving, and he wants to make amends: 'I came back to set things right ... Not just be the sum total of every stupid bloody mistake I've ever made' (2005b:138).

As the rumours spread that the government has supported the training of non-union workers in Dubai and that the Reynolds Company is moving to sack its unionised workers, the tension becomes palpable. There is a sense of disbelief followed by dismay as Reynolds sends in security guards with rottweilers to forcibly remove and lock out 1,400 workers. Matt and Sandy organise a union picket at the Reynolds terminal where they are in for a big fight as they are joined by members of other unions striking in sympathy. In the meantime, the Australian Federal Court is considering whether the members of the MUA have an arguable case that they were unlawfully dismissed for being members of a trade union. As the play draws to a close, the unions win their battle, the striking wharfies return to work, and Sandy gets his dying wish of passing his last weeks at the bush shack with his family gathered around him. They remain a politically un-reconciled group, but they speak of Sandy with admiration as they fulfill his last request for his body to be cremated and his remains tossed to the sea.

Despite the note of gentle optimism sounded by the play's final scene, Thomson does not romanticise the union and its struggle for workers' rights. On the picket line Sandy's mate Frog expresses a desperate rage; he is not emboldened by the strike, instead he feels that what 'we're doing out here is begging. Begging to go in to work and earn a crust ... I don't understand. I wasn't brought up to beg ... This isn't how I thought it would be' (2005b:108). This sense of despair and bewilderment brought about by economic reform lies at the heart of this play. Thomson explains that this particular dispute was:

> a warning bell, it was pre-Tampa , it was pre-September 11 and the anti terrorist legislation, pre-Iraq invasion, and at that time everyone was saying 'they're lying here, the government is lying to us, they had schemed to do this and we don't like it' and we were shocked ... Plus it was evident by the number of people who, if you recall, came in their suits to protest, people who couldn't give a toss about the Union movement, or even didn't like the MUA, they recognised that there was a core value there being attacked, and I thought that was interesting (Thomson 2005a).

Sandy and Frog represent an older generation of workers struggling to come to terms with a new world order which they find inexplicable:

Sandy says, 'You keep pinching yourself to remember you're in Australia. This has happened in Australia' (2005b:85). The implication is that the received idea defining Australian working life, encapsulated in the rhetoric of the fair go, has been swept away in order to make room for a new set of priorities where individualism extinguishes the collective spirit. Thomson documents this fundamental shift in the way working-class Australians have adapted, with varying degrees of success, to the new priorities.

One outcome of the triumph of economic rationalism in Australia is the virtual disappearance of class as a means of understanding the political terrain. Partly the result of a general increase in living standards over the period, it is also a function of the persuasiveness of neo-liberal rhetoric which values individual qualities and actions. This has meant, according to Judith Brett, that 'inequality, deprivation, injustices and oppression had not gone, but class differences no longer seemed … a plausible way of understanding them, and class-based actions no longer a viable way of remedying them' (Brett 2002:190). Thomson's play understands class and class difference; it acknowledges the importance (and plausibility) of a class-based reading of the impact of economic rationalism on Australia. Towards the play's end Sandy is discovered by his family sitting on a park bench and weeping openly, 'not even covering his eyes' (2005b:135). At first it seems that his impending death is the cause of his inconsolable distress, but he is in fact overwhelmed with sadness and a terrible sense of loss as he perceives how the forces of economic rationalism are wearing away the heart of society: 'It's as if we're an inconvenience … we're this sullen swamp they have to keep shifting. Or filling in. Getting in the way of the economy' (2005b:137).

Brett underlines this shift in discourse and philosophy, beginning with Keating's economic reforms in the 1980s and continuing through the period of Howard's government, and argues that economic rationalism came to 'describe the whole gamut of neo-liberal economic reforms designed to increase competition in the economy'. As a term, she says, it captures:

> … something of the puzzlement felt by most Australians as their
> familiar political and economic landscape was changed, seemingly

overnight and despite their wishes. It expressed the sense that much that was valuable in Australian political experience was being swept aside in the name of slogans of dubious wisdom, that the economists had got hold of the reins and were driving us towards a utopia which would turn out to be as misguided and flawed as all past utopias ... (Brett 2002:172).

Thomson's play received mixed reviews. One critic noted that the play made its mark by re-working David Williamson's portrait of Sydney (in his play *Emerald City* (1987)) as 'a makeover metropolis' and refocusing local audiences on Sydney's 'pluckier spirit: its citizens can hunker down when fired by a sense of injustice, and fight' (Fitzgerald 2004). However this critic also says the play 'lacks focus' and only 'skims the dockyard drama'; another reviewer argues that while it is a 'compelling story' the script is 'undercooked' (Fitzgerald 2004; Boland 2004b). In contrast, Fensham and Varney argue that the play makes 'a timely investigation of the strengths and weaknesses' of the culture of unionism (2005:192). In particular, they note that the play 'represents contemporary politics as an epic struggle between the unions and government-backed corporations ...' (2005:196). It is this quality of the work that makes it a pertinent case-study: its specific political content, its topicality and relevance to the current political scene, and its vigorous critique of the forces of neo-liberalism. If the political successes of the Howard government can be partially attributed to its ability to harness economic rationalism to the nationalist Australian legend, Thomson is engaged in a significant counter-discursive strategy. Thomson poses a critical paradox at the heart of the new ideological paradigm; how are the values and priorities of the free market economy to be reconciled with the ethos of egalitarianism and the fair go?

Harbour offers an engaged critique with key issues in the public domain, and uses the theatre as a platform from which to stage its interrogation. It exemplifies political theatre – as defined in the Introduction – because it demonstrates how the political impacts on lived experiences, and offers a critique of the economic policies that shaped them. More broadly, it reveals the ideological frameworks that have seen neo-liberalist discourse and values achieve its hegemonic status in contemporary Australian society.

Who's Afraid of the Working Class?

> *Who's Afraid of the Working Class?* ... a lot of people saw that
> work and were reminded of something they thought had been
> lost, a simple poor theatre. I am making a conscious political
> choice to work in the context of poor theatre (Bovell 2002a).

The play's title, *Who's Afraid of the Working Class?*, immediately
signals its authors' insistence that the notion of class remains an active
and meaningful signifier of difference. This work is an anthology of
plays, developed over a three year period, written by a team, namely:
Andrew Bovell, Patricia Cornelius, Christos Tsiolkas and Melissa
Reeves, with music composed Irene Vela. Bovell explains that it was
important to highlight the subject of class in these plays, partly because
of the way in which it is deemed 'irrelevant':

> There is no doubt that we have been made to feel redundant
> in our preoccupations with class; that it is passé. [Despite
> this view], it's not irrelevant, the only people for whom it's
> irrelevant are the vested interests who don't want to promote
> it as legitimate fare because it will expose something. Class, the
> way it operates in our society, is a subject that needs talking
> about. (Bovell 2002a)

Taken as a whole, *Who's Afraid of the Working Class?* demonstrates
an abiding understanding of class as a critical social category, but it
does not have a triumphalist message about the possibilities for class-
based actions as a means of remedying inequality. Rather, this work
takes an unsentimental look at the lives of people who are the 'losers'
in the newly restructured global economy. As Bovell has described it,
the play depicts the working class as 'disorganised, disempowered and
suffering from a decade of economic rationalism' (Bovell 2006). These
are people who have 'slipped through the net and failed to ride the wave
of aspiration into the middle class' (Bovell 2006). The tearing up of the
social contract has resulted in whole sections of the population being
cast aside, particularly the unemployed, non-white and the working
poor. Importantly, too, the characters in this play are not necessarily
conscious of their marginality – unlike Sandy and the characters in
Harbour who define themselves by means of their class consciousness
and see unionism as a critical mechanism for the expression and

protection of their rights. In *Who's Afraid of the Working Class?* there is no class consciousness, and no industrial framework to help make sense of the political circumstances that proscribe each character's life. This is a portrait of a section of Australian society which has been locked out of participating in the 'mainstream' by the forces of globalisation. Guy Rundle accounts for this sense of dislocation by arguing that many people in this period are 'post-political – not merely alienated, but living in relationship to a macropolitics which categorically excludes public participation'. Echoing Pusey's notion of the social contract, Rundle suggests that where previously the sense of self had been 'anchored to a stable, abiding world of others in a universe of relatively fixed meanings', there now exists in the globalised world the problem of self-integration; 'the problem of how to achieve a meaningful existence ...' (2000:145). This kind of existential questioning, identified by Rundle, is a feature of *Who's Afraid of the Working Class?* – each of the characters do what they can to survive while feeling unanchored or dislocated from the social structures which seem to hold the rest of the world in place.

Who's Afraid of the Working Class? was produced by the Melbourne Workers Theatre and opened at the Victorian Trades Hall in Melbourne on 1 May 1998 in the middle of the Maritime Workers dispute. It was one of the company's most successful shows receiving both popular and critical acclaim.

The play is made up of four parts (each written by a different author), and each part is divided into four or five short scenes which are threaded together so that each story is interwoven with the others. In the story line entitled 'Suit', by Christos Tsiolkas, a young Aboriginal man, Jamie, is trying to make his way in a white world. Jamie is hard-bitten and cynical; he is alienated from both white and black cultures, and as a result he is caught up in a cycle of self-loathing. When we first meet Jamie he is staying in a cheap rural motel, and the prostitute Claire comes to his room. In the scene that follows Jamie humiliates Claire: 'You better wash, white cunt smells, you know? ... It smells like death' (2000:23). He uses money to force her to debase herself which makes him feel sexually aroused and powerful. It is a scene in which complex power relations, inter-cut by tensions around both gender and race, are played out. As a female prostitute, Claire is insulted and degraded in order to earn money. As an Aboriginal man, Jamie feels that he is powerless in a society that routinely insults and degrades him, so he exerts his masculinity and experiences a momentary (and sexualised) rush of power in relation to the white world, as symbolised by Claire. She finally has enough of his goading and, pushed to the limits of her tolerance, throws the money back in his face telling him: 'Boong. Boong … Fucking good-for-nothing black bastard. You filthy, drunk, abo pig …' (2000:27). During this racist tirade Jamie climaxes and then re-offers the money to Claire who takes it and leaves. The ironies here are potent ones; they are in fact both outsiders, both marginalised people who attack each other in a desperate attempt to feel less powerless, and thereby achieve what can only be described as a momentary and pyrrhic victory. Jamie's anger towards the racist society he lives in is turned inward, manifesting itself as a form of debilitating and ultimately disempowering self-loathing.

In the story line 'Money', written by Patricia Cornelius, a man and a woman and their 18-year-old son Daniel are fighting about money. There is not enough to go around, not enough to pay the bills, and there is a sense of desperation about how they will keep their house. Daniel wants money and they fight over some dollars that are missing from the woman's purse. The couple fights about who is to blame for their predicament. The man has lost his job but cannot bear the humiliation of admitting this to his son. There is no love left between this man and woman – it is as if their circumstances have driven away any remnants of tenderness they might have once felt for each other. Cornelius explains:

> When I wrote about money [in the play] and how money affects people, I had a discussion between very ordinary people where money has absolutely worn them down, and so what you hear is a language where people, who were once loving, can now barely stop to give a kiss that's asked for. So we're not ever thinking about the world and money, but we're looking at how it has stripped away anything nice … (Cornelius 2002)

Later, the man sits on a train with his briefcase and starts a conversation with a young woman. At first the man patronises her and tells her she is badly dressed, she looks 'stupid and cheap' (2000:46); he tells her that she won't find a job 'looking like that', and that whatever hopes and dreams she may have for herself will come to nothing. It is a bitter tirade reflecting his own sense of crushing disappointment at his unrelentingly bleak circumstances. The girl gets up and accidentally bumps the man's briefcase which opens to reveal that there is nothing inside. His cover as a respectably employed man on his way to work is blown. She jeers at him and identifies with cruel accuracy that he is a hopeless case, redundant and self-deluding. At the scene's close the man responds to her cruel barbs: 'You're so smart aren't you? At least I had a job. I worked for fifteen years. That's got to mean something. Don't you think?' The girl replies: 'What's it got to mean? Who's it got to mean something to? Who gives a shit?' (2000:49–50)

A number of issues emerge from this scenario. Cornelius depicts the relationship between unemployment and a lack of self respect; the man's sense of self worth is entirely embodied in the definition of himself as a worker. Without this definition he is lost and humiliated, unable to find another way to make sense of the world. Just as Jamie in 'Suit' turns his anger inwards, here too, the unemployed goad and deride each other. There is no place for kindness here because no one can afford to think of anyone but themselves.

In an interview Cornelius expresses a concern about how writing working-class drama can be a voyeuristic experience for middle-class audiences:

> ... the biggest danger is writing slice of life stuff. I am not interested in that ... I feel uncomfortable with looking at the misery of people for its own sake. There's a kind voyeuristic attachment to the under class, that sense of loving a bit of a nasty, dirty, drunken story (Cornelius 2002).

Given these concerns, her dramaturgical strategy is to write dialogue which is repetitive, yet sparse and pared back. The story is told without sentimentality. She describes this kind of unadorned dialogue 'as the way people [really] talk ... quick and hard ... [written with] compassion but with no sentimentality whatsoever' (Cornelius 2002).

In 'Trash', written by Andrew Bovell, a brother and a sister are living on the streets. The boy, Orton, is working as a prostitute to bring in money and food. He ran away from home because his mother's various boyfriends thrashed him and made his life unbearable. His younger sister, Stacey, is thirteen and she has left home to find Orton and bring him back. Stacey reveals to her brother that she has been sexually abused by Nathan, her mother's current boyfriend, but she loves her mum, and wants to fetch Orton home so they can be together again. In order to keep warm at night, the two children sleep in a Brotherhood bin using the clothes as blankets. They light a candle and talk to each other about what life would be like if Orton could find his dad, and Stacey could go home to her mother without Nathan, or any of the other abusive boyfriends, in the house. Later, we meet the children's mother, Rhonda, who has been brought to the morgue to identify the remains of her children who have been burnt to death in the Brotherhood bin. She insists on seeing the bodies and describes how they are: 'all black from the fire and burnt together like one' (2000:69). This appalling story of children abused by a more-or-less uncaring adult world provides one of the key images for the play as a whole. The image of the charred intertwined bodies of these children found in the Brotherhood bin is called-up in the other stories and acts as a linking device between them. It is a potent image of neglect; the neglect of one generation visited upon the next. It is also an image which connotes a shocking end to innocence. This is not a world in which the innocent can survive or the powerless can be protected against the powerful. The writer paints a picture in which poverty and abuse, itself the product of the social and economic alienation of a whole sector of the community, wreaks havoc on the individual and the family in an apparently unbreakable cycle. As Meyrick (the play's director) suggests, this is a play peopled with characters who 'struggle not politically, heroically, resistively, but baldly, personally, in anguish. They struggle not to overcome but simply to stay alive' (2000:4).

In the fourth story 'Dream-Town', written by Melissa Reeves, two 15-year-old schoolgirls are shoplifting. Katina and Trisha are working-class girls from migrant backgrounds; they are lively and funny and prepared to take risks. They have stolen two private school uniforms from Trisha's house where her mother sews uniforms for a living. In a changing room of a department store they put on layers of stolen fancy evening gowns underneath the uniforms and then attempt to leave the store undetected. The entire enterprise is founded on their assumption that private school girls will not be suspected of shoplifting; they don't need to because 'they've got buckets of money' (2000:41), and if Katina and Trisha just 'act rich' as they leave the store, they'll get away with their booty. Later, we discover that they have been caught and are taken to the police station. Here the girls are subject to the interrogations of a policeman who takes objection to their ruse; 'Deception, fraud, trickery, impersonation. All in the same criminal family ... You're not allowed to dress up in other people's clothes ... It's dangerous and confusing. That's what clothes are for, so you can tell everyone apart from everyone else' (2000:70). The girls see this as risible nonsense, but for them it points to a larger truth that they recognise – that class and class difference is a visible phenomenon and they could not successfully 'pass' for rich. These girls are from Coburg, a traditionally working-class ethnic suburb of Melbourne, and the police immediately and accurately identify their class location. This is made apparent when the policeman observes, 'You haven't got much, have you?', and suggests that their attempt to dress up as rich girls is the product of their pathetic envy and anger (2000:76). The policeman taunts the girls with: 'You've got nothing ... you've got nothing'. Trisha replies: 'We haven't got nothing ... We're fucking smart. We know how things operate. We see the inside of things, the messy bitching ugly inside of things, not just the nice things, not just the prettied-up fucking bits. We're fucking smart, so don't you tell us we've got nothing ...' (2000:76). As a statement it is a long way from the proud class consciousness of characters like Sandy in *Harbour*, but it nevertheless expresses a knowingness about the status and capacity of the outsider to see things as they really are. And this, Reeves suggests, takes brains and courage.

In discussing the starting point for the development of *Who's Afraid of the Working Class?*, Bovell explains that the writers and composer were interested in working collaboratively to produce a 'poor' theatre where the simple and unadorned production values throw into relief the boldness of its political themes, and the diversity of its aesthetic ambitions:

I do believe in diversity – politically, ideologically, and aesthetically. I don't see diversity on our main stages; I see the same actors [and] they are invariably white and Anglo-Saxon, and I am not satisfied with that as a portrayal of our culture. I want what is ugly and difficult and doesn't fit in ... Because we are still trying to understand something about ourselves through these pictures we are making (Bovell 2002a).

Who's Afraid of the Working Class? was written and produced when Jeff Kennett was the Premier of Victoria. Kennett was a conservative neo-liberal whose agenda was to boost the performance of the state through a comprehensive program of economic and industrial reforms. This involved opening up the economy to competition and entrepreneurialism and, at the same time, pulling back the role of government as a service provider. In this era the Kennett government contracted out most of the government's activities to competitive tendering, including a raft of social and welfare services. The late 1990s in Victoria was a changed political and economic environment in which 'the social democratic culture of service and equity was replaced by a market culture of competition and consumer choice' (Brett 2002:171–2). Some aspects of this changed political environment are explored in this play. People have lost their jobs due to restructuring and downsizing; men and women have been displaced and made redundant, families struggle to survive without sufficient welfare or support. It is a portrait of a society in which the government has retreated from its social obligations, leaving the marginalised without a voice and without much hope.

It is a measure of the play's sophisticated handling of the complexities of these changes that its opening scene contains a discussion of precisely these issues from the perspective of a young working-class man who idolises Jeff Kennett. In this monologue the young man not only sexually fantasies about Kennett, he tells us why he supports him politically; the boy admires the vigour and strength of Kennett's approach; Kennett's uncompromising stance and his lack of social compassion makes him a 'real man' prepared to show the world how tough he can be:

I love Jeff Kennett. I think he's a good guy, a sexy guy. I like it that he's tall. I like it that he's smart, I like it that he doesn't

> give a shit about anyone . . . He's not whingeing all the time, not
> bludging, not making excuses. He's got style, he looks good and
> he knows it; he's got class. It's written all over him. But, he's not
> soft. He's not soft at all (2000:11).

The boy's monologue sets the tone for the play as a whole which avoids
making the banal assumption that the marginalised and oppressed in
society always act in the interests of their class. This kind of reductive
thinking around the notion of false consciousness is noticeably absent
in the play where, instead, people's values and beliefs are constructed
as complex negotiations involving the intersection of class with gender,
sexuality and race. The boy in this monologue, for example, despite
coming from a traditional working-class and ethnic family, seeks to
align himself with what would appear to be his ideological enemy. But
the boy is not simply a function of his class location. In his analysis
of the play D'Cruz points out that the boy's identity is made up of a
complex interplay of factors: he is gay, a migrant and deeply attracted
to the style of aggressive machismo. D'Cruz argues that: 'These
characteristic traits point to the poverty of traditional class analysis
because the boy's place in the production process, or his father's place
in the production process, does not necessarily imply any specific form
of political consciousness ... there is no necessary connection between
the character's class position and his politics because the discourses,
institutions and desires that shape his subjectivity — the discourse of
Machismo ... his homosexuality — cannot be reduced to the logic of
the economy' (D'Cruz 2005:210). Thus while the play can be seen
as a specific response to the politics of the era and a critique of the
economic policies that shaped it, it also makes a contribution to the
much broader task of teasing out the ideological frameworks that have
seen neo-liberalist discourse and values achieve its hegemonic status in
contemporary Australian society.

  Bovell is clearly aware of the potential difficulties of producing
such an unrelentingly bleak picture of Australian society as he and the
other writers have done in *Who's Afraid of the Working Class?*. In a
rhetorical mode, he asks the question: 'Why would you pay money
to be confronted by poverty, loneliness, alienation and despair?'
(Bovell 2006). But as he points out, such aspects of life have 'been the

stuff of drama since Aristotle and Shakespeare' (Bovell 2006). More importantly, he argues, this is theatre which is intended to provoke and challenge Australian audiences:

> I think Australian audiences do want to laugh and sometimes they want to forget and the theatre shouldn't disappoint them. But I don't think all of the audience wants to do that all of the time ... I continue to believe that enough of us want and expect our theatre to take on the difficult issues of the times, to tell the hard stories and to scrutinise our culture and politics and way of life (Bovell 2006).

The plays discussed in this chapter, each with its own emphasis, have addressed the 'difficult issues of our time' and have told the hard stories. In particular, they have looked at the rise of neo-liberalism in Australia as a means of articulating a critique of the nation. They have understood the development over the past decade of a persuasive rhetoric of individualism and choice, and the equating of liberty with the 'market contract'. Each of these plays documents the deterioration of social liberalist philosophy which, as Sawer and Pusey argued, historically formed the basis of key Australian institutions, practices and beliefs. Thomson, Bovell, Reeves, Tsiolkas and Cornelius have written very different plays ranging in style and subject matters. However, they share a fascination with political processes and, in particular, with understanding the changing moral and ideological frameworks engendered by the domination of neo-liberalism in Australia.

Geraldine Turner as the Mother in the 2003 Sydney Theatre Company production of *These People*. (Photo: Heidrun Löhr)

CHAPTER 5

FORTRESS AUSTRALIA

In his great work analysing Australian film narratives, Graeme Turner says: 'Nationalism is an ideology and its cultural function is not to define Australia as a real entity but to represent Australia as an ideological construction' (1986:122). Providing an ideological reading of the ways in which nationalism has been constructed and deployed in Australia has been a project of many scholars. Ann Curthoys (2000), for example, has shown how popular historical mythologies have stressed the struggles and courage of the settler period as a means of masking Australia's racist past. Marilyn Lake (1997; 2000) has addressed the historically gendered aspects of nationalism; while James Jupp questions the claim for overarching values and cultural uniqueness by examining the ways in which national identity has been reshaped by Australian immigration (1997; 2000). Such studies repudiate the notion of a single national identity either as historical fact or as a politically desirable goal. Like Turner's research into Australian narratives, they emphasise the fundamentally political nature of identity discourses.

Multiculturalism has been central to debates over questions of history and identity in Australia since it was first mooted in 1973 by Al Grassby, the Minister for Immigration in the Whitlam Labor government. The succeeding Liberal government led by Malcolm Fraser established a policy of multiculturalism and created the Institute for Multicultural Affairs. As an official policy, it involved:

> ... the public acceptance of immigrant and minority groups as distinct communities, which are distinguishable from the majority population with regard to language, culture and social behaviour, and which have their own associations and social infrastructure (Castles 2001).

The Fraser government also significantly boosted Asian immigration although its successor the Hawke Labor government subsequently cut the intake because of high unemployment. Nevertheless the overall proportion of Asian refugees settling in Australia continued to rise because a family reunion program for Vietnamese refugees remained in place (Kelly 1992:129). Immigration became an item on the public agenda when a perceived over-representation of Asians in the immigration mix prompted the historian Geoffrey Blainey to raise concerns about immigration policies in 1984. He argued that the immigration policies of the day were detrimental to social cohesion and homogeneity which were factors in maintaining a stable political and social order: 'The multicultural policy, and its emphasis on what is different and on the rights of the new minority rather that the old majority, gnaws at that sense of solidarity that many people crave for' (Blainey 1984:153). Blainey's controversial critique goes to the heart of the difficulty faced by leaders of all political persuasions in Australia as they attempted to reconcile the objectives of ethnic diversity with national unity. James Curran argues that Blainey's comments reflected a 'growing disquiet' amongst political conservatives that the rhetoric of multiculturalism and Aboriginal injustice was a catalyst for undermining traditional beliefs in the pioneering achievements of the white settlers – achievements that had been a source of national pride (2004:173).

Both multiculturalism and the Blainey debate about immigration were part of the process by which the traditional definitions of national identity were made more complex and multi-dimensional from the 1980s onwards. They also provided a critical context within which the theatre began to explore multicultural themes, stories, images and experiences.

Multiculturalism in the Theatre

In the 1980s the Australia Council was seen as one of a number of government agencies which could 'foster ethnic diversity' (Johanson 2000:159). The support for artists and organisations from Non-English-Speaking backgrounds (NESB) was part of a wider argument for social justice and equity which informed policy development in the community arts sector. As Gibson has noted, multicultural arts challenged the dominant rationale of government funding to support excellence and encouraged instead the adoption of 'culturally pluralist' strategies (Gibson 2001:112).

As the implications of multiculturalism were being worked through by the Australia Council, theatre practices exploring multiculturalism were evident around the country. In Adelaide, for example, the theatre work of *Doppio Teatro* specifically acknowledged the Italian–Australian migrant experience. Using a mixture of professional and non-professional actors, the company produced multi-lingual and community-based work which celebrated the cultural distinctiveness of its community such as the 1989 work *Ricordi* which told the personal stories of women migrants. The production, which successfully toured Adelaide, Sydney and Melbourne, evoked personal memories of home and the sense of dispossession felt by these women on their arrival in Australia (Sutton 1989:36).

Despite great diversity in content and style, Tompkins identifies a number of 'signifiers' shared by much multicultural theatre: 'storytelling; the use of English and at least one other language; and representation of "home"' (Tompkins 1998). *The Journey* written by Tes Lyssiotis and produced at the Wharf Theatre in Sydney in 1987 addressed the experience of migrants arriving in Australia, and their survival in a migrant detention centre outside Albury. A multilingual performance (actors spoke in Italian, English, Greek and German), the play looked at three couples each having migrated from different countries and living together in cramped conditions in a Nissen hut.

Multicultural theatre was not confined to writers from migrant communities. *Mary* (1982), researched and written by Hannie Rayson for Theatreworks, addressed the experience of second generation migrants in Melbourne's eastern suburbs where the theatre company was based at that time. *Mary* initially played in local schools and subsequently received a series of main-stage productions (at the Playbox and then the Universal Theatre) followed by an interstate tour from 1981. In the play Mary, a second generation adolescent Greek girl makes friends with her adolescent Anglo neighbour. Like other plays within the genre it is based on research and documentation. Rayson comments:

> I did research with kids from Doncaster East secondary school
> to familiarise myself with the teenage vernacular and concerns.
> I also chose a suburb which had had a big influx of Greeks ... [I
> interviewed] students from the high school ... and then there
> was a Greek youth group that I met with, and then I met a lot
> of individual people as well ... (Rayson 2005a).

The work met the goals of the Australia Council's policy priorities of
the era – its development through community consultation emphasised
inclusivity, access and participation. Further, the play underwrote the
idea that the 'Australian experience' did not simply mean the stories
and perspectives of white and Anglo-Saxon Australians; it now implied
something broader. In the case of *Mary* the focus was now on the
perspectives of young migrant women. Rayson comments:

> I had hoped that [for migrants and their children] the play spoke
> the truth [about] their problems and their aspirations and their
> circumstances, that it was authentic in as much as it captured
> their language and the way they thought about things ... And
> the effect of that would be to ... empower them because their
> stories had been heard. And for kids who were Anglos, that
> it might broaden their understanding because [the play gave]
> a more intimate glimpse of what it was like to see the world
> through other's eyes. I hoped it would have a warm embrace
> for women generally because it was about mother–daughter
> relationships (Rayson 2005a).

Rayson says that at the time it was unusual to have a main-stage play
looking at multicultural issues and that the production of *Mary*,
along with the flourishing of other multicultural theatre, helped to
build a new audience for this work. Certainly the decade saw a huge
growth in the production of multicultural theatre. Mitchell describes
the late 1980s as a time when the 'outpouring of expression' from
Non-English-Speaking Backgrounds (NESB) artists reached its peak
(Mitchell 1998:132). Indeed, the production of work by companies
such as *Doppio Teatro* in Adelaide and Filiki Players in Melbourne,
demonstrated a growing tendency for NESB artists to take the
multicultural agenda out of the hands of Anglo-Australian artists
(such as Rayson) in the interests of cultural integrity and authenticity.
Their success demonstrates how the access and equity policies of the

Australia Council in the 1980s provided opportunities for new work from new artists to emerge.

This phenomenon is perhaps best exemplified in the hit production *Wogs Out of Work* which started life as a small one-off production for the 1987 Melbourne Comedy Festival. It grew to become one of the most successful theatre productions of the 1980s and was eventually seen by an estimated 500,000 people, many of whom had never been to the theatre before. Devised and performed by Nick Giannopoulos, Simon Palomares and Maria Portesi, the show reclaimed the derogatory term 'wog' and turned it into a celebratory self-definition. At the same time it critiqued the political appropriation of multiculturalism which reduced 'difference' to exotic images of the 'other'.

The theatre of the 1980s, then, was characterised by a new diversity in stories, styles and subject matters providing a re-reading of national identity to incorporate a more pluralist ethos. This is particularly apparent in the areas of community arts and multiculturalism where new theatre practices emerged which challenged the theatre of the New Wave, repudiating its largely monocultural reading of national character.

Following Blainey's attack on the issue of Asian migration in the mid-1980s, multiculturalism was again the focus of public attention after 1996 as a result of the rising public profile of the conservative Queensland independent politician, Pauline Hanson and her One Nation Party. In her maiden speech to parliament in 1996 Hanson said: 'if I can invite whom I want into my home, then I should have the right to have a say in who comes into my country' (Hanson 1996). She argued that Australia was 'in danger of being swamped by Asians' and called for multiculturalism to be abolished (Hanson 1996).

In 2001 racial tensions in Australia came to the fore – tensions which focused on the particular issue of Muslim and Arab migration and aroused widespread public anxiety about race and multiculturalism. In August there was the Tampa incident: a boatload of Afghan refugees rescued by a Norwegian cargo ship was refused entry to Australia and the Howard government used naval force to repel them. Maritime border control, which up until 2001 had been focused on stemming the entry of illegal Asian refugees, was now protecting Australia from a flood of unwanted Muslim refugees. The justification for using an armed defence force against refugees required the government to persuade the Australian public that these refugees were desperate, disreputable and undeserving of sanctuary. The effort to produce a generalised suspicion of Muslims was a significant strategy of the government and it was largely successful. As Robert Manne has pointed out, it was the reason why 'the story of Iraqis, on a later boat, throwing their children into the ocean as a form of moral blackmail was so readily given credence' (Manne 2006:39).

Following Tampa, in September 2001, al-Qaeda's attack on the World Trade Centre in New York prompted a US-led 'war on terror'. Australia joined with its American ally to send troops to Afghanistan and Iraq, while Iraqi and Afghani refugees continued to attempt to arrive in Australia. Many of them were fleeing persecution but they were often seen by the media as a terrorist threat, and dubbed as 'illegals' or 'queue jumpers' (Marr & Wilkinson 2003:30). Playwright Michael Gurr captured the irony of this situation: 'The government is imprisoning and defaming people who have fled from countries we think are places worth escaping from. The language has been expertly hijacked. Illegals. Queue-jumpers. There is nothing illegal about seeking asylum and there are no queues to join in Afghanistan' (Gurr 2006:76).

Poynting argues that since the mid-1990s in Australia the Middle Eastern/Muslim 'other' has been constructed through the media's portrayal of desperate asylum seekers as 'backward, uncivilised, irrational, violent, criminally inclined, misogynistic ... a whole litany of evil attributes' (Poynting 2006:89). This demonisation of the Muslim in Australia is portrayed in Michael Futcher and Helen Howard's play *A Beautiful Life* (1998). The play tells the story of Hamid and Jhila – Iranian refugees who, after settling in Australia in the 1980s, are driven to protest against the human rights atrocities taking place in their homeland. The play is loosely based on a real-life event: in 1992 at the Iranian embassy in Canberra a group of Iranian refugees staged a peaceful protest which suddenly turned violent. In the play, Hamid and Jhila participate in the protest, get caught up in the ensuing violence and are then arrested on suspicion of terrorism. The play addresses a number of issues: human rights abuse, the complicity of the West in supporting the corrupt political regimes of the Middle East, the treatment of refugees in Australia and the general suspicion of those from Middle Eastern backgrounds. Futcher and Howard are alert to the multiple ironies in this scenario which sees those escaping terrorism being tarred with the same brush as their persecutors. Hamid and Jhila are accused of being involved in a terrorist incident but, as the lawyer Stephanie explains: 'they are opposed to terrorism! That's why they were allowed into Australia in the first place' (Futcher & Howard 2000:39). Written a year before September 11 and the Tampa crisis, the play is prescient in its portrayal of the difficulties that have continued to face Muslim refugees in Australia. It sees Australia as a place divided into 'us' and 'them': 'ordinary Australians' versus the Arab 'other' perpetually under suspicion as agents of global terror.

Nikos Papastergiadis has expounded a theory that government policy in relation to the refugee crisis is shaped by an 'invasion complex' involving the construction of the figure of the Muslim/Arab refugee as 'the harbinger of global chaos and terror ... an agent of disruption' (2004:16). This targeting of the Muslim 'other' has intensified during the US-led 'war on terror' and appears to provide support for the argument for ongoing involvement in the war in Iraq.

In the light of such developments, Ghassan Hage and Ien Ang have deepened their analysis of Australian national identity to look at the impact of multiculturalism. They demonstrate that the discussion of nationalism is intricately bound up with issues of race and cultural identity. Ang provides a means of deconstructing hegemonic readings of nationalism through an analysis of what she calls 'fortress Australia'; an anxious desire to 'maintain a closely guarded boundary around Australia as a separate nation-state' (Ang 2003:53). Multiculturalism, says Ang, has been seen as an ideological challenge to the notion of a united and singular national identity such that 'in Howard's mind, multiculturalism is always in tension with "the national interest"' (2003:65). Thus, the notion of 'fortress Australia' has been evidenced most clearly by the border protection strategies of the Howard government and the corresponding asylum seeker detention policies. This is a key issue for how the nation is understood and discussed in a number of theatre productions as well as films, documentaries and a television drama dealing with the plight of refugees and asylum-seekers that have emerged since 2001.

Actors for Refugees have presented productions which dramatised the experiences of refugees for schools and community groups since September 2001. In 2002 they performed *Kan Yama Kan* (*Once Upon a Time*), a documentary-style work using verbatim accounts of asylum seekers as a way of highlighting their plight. In 2003 Actors for Refugees staged a moving tribute to the harrowing experience of Amal Hasan Basri, an Iraqi woman who survived the sinking of the SIEV X: a boat loaded with refugees which sank off Ashmore reef (in waters between Indonesia and Australia) in October 2001 causing the deaths of 353 asylum seekers, most of them Iraqis. This documentary theatre piece entitled *Something to Declare* was written by Michael Gurr and performed at the Melbourne Town Hall, followed by subsequent productions around the country. In writing this documentary drama, Gurr notes: 'There seems no need to imagine a refugee. Any story a writer could come up with is put immediately in the shadows by the plain facts' (Gurr 2006:78). In 2005, Performing Lines produced the play, *Through the Wire*, written and directed by Ros Horin, which used the accounts of four Iranian and Iraqi refugees to paint an intimate picture of their lives behind the razor wire of Australia's detention centres.

Film and television productions grappled with similar issues. In 2003 the documentary, *Molly & Mobarak* looked at the lives of a group of Afghani refugees in rural Australia. In the same year, the ABC screened John Doyle's two-part drama *Marking Time*, which exposed the difficulties facing refugees in Australia – a story told through the relationship between an Afghani girl and an Australian boy. A feature length documentary, *Letters to Ali*, made by Clara Law and Eddie Fong, looking at the consequences of the government's detention of an Afghani child, was released in 2004.

Other plays which have addressed the issue of asylum seeker policies are Ben Ellis' *These People* (2003) and Hannie Rayson's *Two Brothers* (2005). Their dramatic exploration of this issue provides a critique of 'fortress Australia' as part of the hegemonic definition of nationhood.

Rayson's play was subjected to an eviscerating commentary from conservative newspaper columnist Andrew Bolt, and this chapter also analyses the nature of his attack.

These People

In 2003, Ellis' play *These People* (2003) received a production at the STC as part of its Blueprints program, an initiative of Sydney Theatre Company's Artistic Director Robyn Nevin, which provides workshopping and skill development opportunities for emerging playwrights. *These People*, highlighting the responses of 'ordinary' Australians to the stories of asylum seekers and refugees, was shortlisted for the Community Relations Commission Award at the NSW Premier's Literary Awards (Ellis 2004).

These People is an explicitly political critique of government refugee policies. The idea that the theatre might be the place for trenchant political analysis and discussion is a key one for Ellis: 'politics is a subject [for theatre], and politics is an excuse for theatre almost … Excuse and reason at the same time. Obviously not just political plays – they are plays first of all' (Ellis 2005).

He is wary of the idea of theatre as 'message'. However, at the same time, Ellis does see theatre as having a social and political function:

> I like the idea of being a public facilitator … the stage being some kind of point where the truth can be pursued … The theatre feels like a place where you can actually pursue truths. You might not get the whole truth but you might get glimpses of it … That's definitely something that draws me to the theatre (Ellis 2005).

Ellis also has a commitment to producing theatre which simultaneously entertains and politicises its audiences. Ellis comments:

> I think [the idea of] entertainment is really interesting; plays should be entertaining. Audiences are not stupid either. Audiences can entertain ideas and political messages as much as they can be entertained by [theatre] … it's a two way process … All theatre educates, good theatre entertains (Ellis 2005).

With *These People*, for example, while Ellis had used the Tampa crisis as a starting point, he says he was also concerned to make a theatre piece looking at the public response to refugees which was 'entertaining without being lighthearted' (Clark 2003). One critic confirmed Ellis' achievement noting that this play combines moral passion and outrage with a 'gleeful feeling for the absurd' (McCallum 2003).

For Ellis, one of the key politicising functions of his theatre work is its engagement with generational issues. Ellis articulates a concern with the voicelessness and disempowerment of youth in the face of a domineering and culturally oppressive older generation. He acknowledges the work of cultural theorist Mark Davis who has argued that Australia is riven by a generational 'backlash against young people and the way they think' (Davis 1997:vii). This signal idea has informed a number of Ellis' plays. In *Post Felicity* (2002), for example, the character of Felicity never appears: 'she's been spoken for without ever having had the chance to speak back. And that's how a lot of people in my bracket feel' (Ellis 2005). He describes the generational divide:

> [It's] like a nucleus of a cell ... There's a whole bunch of people in there and they decide what is going to go on for the rest of the cell, but they can't ever allow anything else past this membrane, and [you] feel like you are on the outside of that nucleus, [that feeling is] a characteristic of mine, it's probably a characteristic of most of my generation (Ellis 2005).

To this end, he says, his objective is to write plays where audiences experience other voices, plays which allow audiences:

> ... to recognise there are actually other humans out there who deserve consideration in what we do daily and how we think about politics and how we think about all the other issues that go into public life, that's what I want to happen (Ellis 2005).

In *These People*, Ellis uses a white suburban Australian family to explore issues of immigration and detention. He contrasts the ephemeral middle-class concerns of the Australian family with the life and death struggles of people held in detention centres. The middle-class daughter muses about whether the 'dirty hair look' will suit her, while at the same time a girl at the detention centre has to queue for a bar of soap. The son is eating less as he spends his time partying and taking drugs, while a boy in the detention centre goes on a hunger strike. The acts of self-harm (such as lip sewing) performed by detained refugees as a marker of their feeling of powerlessness over their own bodies

– is less meaningful to the mother in this white Australian family than her anxiety over her son's masturbation habits. The family unit is seen to form a protective barrier against the harsh realities of life in contemporary Australia; and from inside its protective shell, family members cannot recognise the taken-for-granted nature of their values and beliefs. The mother expresses fear, ignorance and middle-class anxiety when she suggests that:

> The whole country needs its stomach stapled. Too many people. It's bursting with struggles and languages and obesity. That's what border protection is about. A national diet (Ellis 2004:22).

The cracks soon appear in the family façade as the son admits: 'It's lonely in there, amongst the family. But it makes you who you are, the family, doesn't it?' (2004:17). This ultimately is Ellis' concern: the family, in this conceit, stands for the nation and it produces individuals who are frightened of difference, and who learn that the most expedient strategy in difficult times is to look out, not for one another, but for oneself. As one critic noted, Ellis' subject here is the 'fantastic charade of suburbia' in which 'self satisfaction and wilful ignorance contend for dominance' (McCallum 2003). In his work Ellis plays with two different versions of the family – in *Falling Petals* there is the deconstruction of the idea of the family as a haven, whereas in these *These People*, the family is a haven of sorts; it is a self-protective and sealed universe blocking out the realities of the world outside. In both versions, Ellis suggests, there are terrible social costs, costs which are effectively masked by persistent hegemonic discourses about the apparently moral virtues of the suburban Australian family.

Reviews of the play noted that it was stylistically uneven, but significant for its satirical take on Australian attitudes to the suffering of detainees and refugees. One critic noted that the play's achievement was its rendering of the power of disconnection: 'the way we abstract distant suffering … Australia is big enough to allow the fancy that our inland camps are actually somewhere else. Not here. Not us' (Dunne 2003b). Writing for the *Australian*, John McCallum praised the play for its 'fearfully apocalyptic vision of a country that has turned its back on humanity and lost its soul' (McCallum 2003). This idea that the government's asylum seeker and refugee detention policies has signalled a fundamental moral shift in Australian values, is also taken up by Hannie Rayson in her 2005 play, *Two Brothers*.

Two Brothers

Jointly commissioned by the MTC and STC, Rayson's play *Two Brothers* (2005b), directed by Simon Phillips, caused a major controversy when it opened in Melbourne in 2005. The play tells the story of two ambitious brothers – Tom and James Benedict. Tom is the head of an Australian community aid organisation and a tireless campaigner for the rights of refugees. His brother, James 'Eggs' Benedict is Minister for Home Securities, a Liberal Party front bencher angling for the top job as Prime Minister. Both brothers are charismatic and impassioned, and both are equally convinced of the rightness of their diametrically opposed views of the world. Eggs is married to Fiona, a despairing woman since the drugs-related death, a few years earlier, of her eldest son Marty. Their younger son Lachlan is an officer with the Australian Navy currently engaged in protecting Australian borders from the incursions of illegal asylum seekers. Tom is married to Ange, a high school teacher, with whom he has a son Harry, an unemployed architect. Together this cast of characters play out the different sides of one of the key debates of contemporary Australian politics.

The explicit political context for the play is made apparent through its exploration of issues around current refugee, asylum-seeker and mandatory detention policies. At a family Christmas gathering we overhear Eggs' phone call with his son Lachlan who is on duty aboard an Australian navy frigate; Lachlan reports that an Indonesian fishing boat, the *Kelepasan*, with hundreds of refugees on board is sinking and urgent assistance is required. Eggs orders him and his company to not provide any assistance, and thus a terrible tragedy occurs with all but one of the refugees drowning. The dramatic presentation of the sinking of the *Kelepasan* and the events which followed is delivered as an eye-witness account by Hazem Al Ayad, the sole survivor of the disaster. It is clearly reminiscent of the factual event of the capsizing of the SIEV X. The government's handling of the SIEV X issue, and the Tampa crisis two months earlier were critical elements in the election campaign fought at the end of 2001 which saw the return of the Howard government. The deaths which resulted from these incidents proved no impediment to the re-election of the Liberal Party. In this play Rayson explores the mindset of a politician who not only catalyses a tragedy through deliberate inaction, but sees his own personal mission to become Prime Minister as reason enough to rationalise the gross moral turpitude of his behaviour. With his astute young policy advisor, Jamie Savage, Eggs produces a media-savvy 'spin' on this event, insisting that his motivations are lofty and patriotic, being based on the self-evident need to protect Australian borders from a potentially unstoppable influx of undesirable elements.

But Rayson seeks to further ensnare her protagonist in a moral quagmire. The sole survivor of the *Kelepasan*, Hazem Al Ayad, who has seen his wife and children drown in the Indian Ocean, is now seeking asylum in Australia. Hazem's appeal to Australian immigration is represented by Tom Benedict who attempts to persuade his hard-line brother that Hazem's case deserves a humanitarian approach. But Hazem is a potential risk to Eggs as he insists that he saw an Australian naval vessel in the water which did not come to the aid of the sinking boat; this is information which Eggs does not want broadcast for fear it will damage his political career. With his appeal rejected by Eggs, Hazem fears being forcibly repatriated to Iraq. Tom sends Hazem to wait for him at the family beach house but, in the middle of the night, Eggs arrives unexpectedly and mistakes Hazem for an intruder. A struggle ensues and Eggs kills Hazem by repeatedly stabbing him with a fishing knife.

In the play, Eggs' overweening ambition to secure the job of Prime Minister enables him to overlook and rationalise his role in the events leading to the sinking of the *Kelepasan*, and his murder of Hazem, as a matter of political necessity. Some of the critical response to the play found this element of skullduggery and high drama so implausible and over the top that it distracted from the play's broader political objectives. For Rayson, the political objective of the play is to deconstruct the operations of power to show how political decision-making is often founded on the premise that the end does indeed justify the means. Eggs is of the view that he took the action that had to be taken to defend Australia the unwanted incursions of refugees with doubtful claims to refugee status. In this way, Eggs attempts to blur the distinction between his own ambition and his apparently disinterested role as protector of the nation's borders which requires him to do an unpalatable but necessary job. He is the patriotic servant of necessity. By tracing the strategy by which Eggs manipulates both the *Kelepasan* disaster and the murder of Hazem for his own political ends, Rayson demonstrates her interest in understanding how the powerful rationalise their power.

The writer John Birmingham has written about the connection between the explicit manipulation of national myth and political outcomes in his account of the Howard government's ideological agenda (Birmingham 2005). In much the same way Rayson is concerned to adumbrate the way in which the Right has redefined 'essential' Australian values as essentially conservative values. In his speech of triumph at the play's end, Eggs sees his victory as confirmation of the twin verities of Australian democracy, a free market and a fair go, a one-line encapsulation of the harnessing of neo-liberalist belief to nationalist rhetoric. Egg's reading of the world is defined by an energetic (if not zealous) individualism, while Tom's humanitarianism is seen by his brother as not only naïve but anachronistic and out-of-step with contemporary Australian political realities and values. Rayson describes her initial motivation for exploring these issues as emerging from a desire to: ' ... understand why right wing politics is on the ascendance ... I want to understand how the values associated with conservatism – self interest, individualism, commitment to the free market – are giving the Right a sense of vigour and energy' (Glow 2005:334).

Eggs believes he has a genuine social role to play, an understanding which manifests itself in his attitude to his children. Like many of Rayson's major plays, parenting is an important feature here. In this play, as in *Life After George* and *Inheritance*, Rayson reads the parent–child relationship as a metaphor for the relationship between the past and the future and the nature of political/social change. In *Life After George*, the eponymous protagonist is a charismatic idealist academic who has unwittingly alienated the children from his first marriage

Garry McDonald as Eggs, Caroline Brazier as Jamie and Nicholas Eadie as Tom in the 2005 Sydney Theatre Company/Melbourne Theatre Company production of *Two Brothers*. (Photo: Jeff Busby)

who feel they can not live up to his expectations and, as a result, can articulate only a sense of cynicism and estrangement. But we know at the play's denouement that George's *raison d'être* has been to pass on to his children his idealism, a sense of optimism about the future, so that they might go on, as he did, fired up by the possibility of changing the world. This sense of a moral contract between parents and children is further explored in *Inheritance* where Dibs attempts to prevent the telling of a dark secret. In the process she betrays her adopted Aboriginal child, and so we understand how the nation betrays its Indigenous population by denying the truth about our shared history. In both these cases Rayson uses the generational differences in a family as a way of dramatising historical and political change, and the moral responsibilities that one generation owes to the next.

In *Two Brothers* Eggs reveals a revulsion for what he sees as weakness and lack of initiative in his sons. There is here a direct corollary with his understanding of his public role as a politician; his 'service' to the public is grounded in a belief in the need to 'be tough' – tough on crime, drugs and asylum seekers. The rhetoric of 'being tough' (and the principles which underlie it) is in opposition to the philosophical basis of social liberalism, or more particularly the welfare state. Sawer analyses this kind of political discourse by arguing that 'gendered metaphors' have developed around contrasting ideas of the state so that 'the gender of the minimal state has almost always been masculine ... [with] values of independence, self-reliance and competitiveness' (Sawer 2004:86). On the other hand, the welfare state, a product of social liberalism, is often seen as female, representing the importance of more caring values in the public sphere. Such a gendered analysis of opposing political stances brings insight to understanding the right-wing view of the world, exemplified by Eggs, with its emphasis on machismo and toughening-up. Eggs blames his wife Fiona for having been too soft on their son Marty who died of a drug overdose, and in the same vein sees his brother's support for refugees as a function of his softness, his 'bleeding heart'. Sawer argues that this kind of neo-liberalist thinking stems from the view that there is something emasculating about the ethical or welfare state (2004:102). Certainly Eggs privileges a self-reliant masculinity as his *modus operandi* both in the public sphere as the successful right-wing politician, and in the private sphere as a husband, father, uncle and brother.

While Eggs privileges the values of self-reliance and competition, his brother Tom has an altogether more humanitarian, social-liberalist approach to the world. Rayson examines how stridently oppositional political allegiances can occur within one family. In writing *Two Brothers* Rayson explained:

> I'm interested in looking at the things that help shape someone's political loyalty, and as always I'm taken up with the intersection of the public and the private. The question of what happens when people play out their personal and ideological views on the public stage, is of great interest to me (Glow 2005:334).

To achieve this Rayson has constructed her two protagonists as significant public figures whom we see from the perspective of the hothouse of one family. Family life is a focus in many of Rayson's plays (for example *Inheritance, Life After George, Hotel Sorrento*), and in each case, the mapping of family dynamics provides the vehicle for an intensive dramatic exploration of the characters' private lives, emotions and personal ambivalences. But Rayson is never interested in the personal for its own sake; rather, her plays offer an investigation of the negotiations that take place between the external political world of actions and behaviours, and the internal private realm of values and beliefs. Rayson is always drawn to the dynamic relationship between the things we believe and the things we do – a tense and often contradictory relationship which, according to Terry Eagleton, defines the nature of ideology (Eagleton 1997:37).

The plays discussed in this chapter bespeak a concern for the apparent repudiation of multiculturalism over the past decade. The chief message of multiculturalism, as it was expressed through the theatre of the 1980s, was the importance of valuing difference. Cultural difference was seen as something that redefined the Australian national image. As the writer Christos Tsiolkas puts it:

> In the early eighties there was racism but ... there was a bipartisan acceptance of ... multiculturalism. Back then I would have said that multiculturalism was a shared Australian value (Tsiolkas 2006:13).

From the mid-1990s, however, there has been a gradual withdrawal from the priorities and goals of multiculturalism. Signalling this shift in 2007 the Howard government re-branded its Department of Immigration and Multiculturalism with the new title Department of Immigration and Citizenship. Such changes are, arguably, an indication of the currency of 'fortress' mentality: a form of what Hage calls 'paranoid nationalism'. This is a nationalism which is founded on an 'obsession with border politics' itself the product of the diminishing of 'societal hope' (Hage 2003:47). The writers discussed here see the government's refugee policies and the concomitant demonizing of the Arab 'other' in these terms. With its repudiation of multiculturalism and the reduction of societal hope, the government is seeking to promote a one nation story with an apparently universalised set of Australian values. Tsiolkas maintains that with the repudiation of the principles of multiculturalism, intolerance becomes 'mandated and acceptable' (Tsiolkas 2006:13). He insists that it is the responsibility of artists to tackle the subject of race and racism in Australia – and this has certainly been the mission of the theatre artists discussed here.

Tsiolkas also argues that in this period racism has been 'argued for seriously in our press and on our television screens'. As an example of this Ghassan Hage describes the racist 'logic' of the media's representation of Muslims as 'a community of people always predisposed towards crime, rape, illegal entry to Australia and terrorism' (Hage 2003:67–8). Furthermore, there is some evidence to suggest that the media has played a role in attacking those who publicly critique government policy. In particular, right-wing media commentators have taken to task those who have expressed an oppositional view on detention and border protection policies. As Michael Gurr has noted: 'The treatment of asylum seekers is something that sends a certain kind of columnist into a frenzy' – a frenzy of specious rhetoric which would have one believe that 'honest battlers want the boats towed back to sea and hyper-educated chatterers want to buy all the queue-jumpers a latte' (Gurr 2006:254). The right-wing media – described by Gurr as 'the government's foot soldiers in the culture wars' (2006:255) – have been active in issuing warnings that those who publicly dissent from government policy are not simply oppositional but expressly 'un-

Australian'. This was the experience of Hannie Rayson. One of the striking features of the production of *Two Brothers* at the MTC in 2005 was that it caused a widespread public response, in particular across the pages of the print media, where several articles repeatedly drew attention to the play's take on refugee and asylum seeker policies.

The Media Response to *Two Brothers*

Two Brothers was by no means the first attempt by an artist to address refugee issues in a critical manner. Yet other plays and documentaries that contained implicit or explicit critiques of refugee policies did not receive the same level of critical attention. What distinguished Rayson's play from the others was that it was produced in and by one of Australia's flagship mainstream theatre companies. The wide reach of mainstream theatre makes it an important site to investigate precisely because it draws in writers who seek to influence public debate. The evidence that they are successful in doing so is borne out by the reception of Rayson's play.

Amongst the responses to *Two Brothers* some significant aesthetic critiques were offered by reviewers and commentators. Some of these reviewers argued that Rayson had painted a picture that was too black and white, too simplistic and melodramatic in its portrait of the battle between the evil and the good brother, and this detracted from the drama's force. Others were concerned about the play's account of the drowning of asylum seekers while the Australian navy stood by and watched. It was argued that since the play was clearly based on the historical event of the sinking of the SIEV X, the playwright had a responsibility to record these events accurately. By failing to do so Rayson had actually done a disservice to the debate around refugee and asylum issues. The play was further attacked as leftist propaganda; a one-sided and one-dimensional account of the politics of the issue and the government of the day. Rayson responded to these criticisms in an article in the *Age* stating that the job of the playwright is not to write investigative journalism, but fiction: 'I chose to write a political thriller – a form of entertainment that looks cruelty, ambition and injustice in the face ... This is dense moral territory. Just the stuff of theatre' (Rayson 2005c). She defended herself from the accusation of being a propagandist by arguing that it is the right and proper function of theatre to interrogate the 'fundamental values' of those in power.

Andrew Bolt

The most heated response to Rayson's play came in a series of articles from conservative *Herald Sun* newspaper columnist, Andrew Bolt. This response is important to document: firstly, it highlights the way the theatre can be a participant in public discussion and the playwright's role in stirring up debate; secondly it exemplifies something of the nature of current public debate. Both David Marr and Guy Rundle have described the discursive use of the term 'elites' to condemn those social 'pathogens': the cultural producers who speak out against government actions. Branding your opponent's political views as those of an elite is a way of refusing to engage with them and a way of excluding them. Rundle argues that it is usually a prelude to more forceful forms of repression such as, perhaps, an anti-terrorism bill with a sedition clause. Bolt's attack on *Two Brothers*, as outlined below, demonstrates not just the ideology of social conservatism and its discursive strategies, but also a rejection of the critical nationalism which Rayson's play evinces.

The day before the play opened, on the 12 April 2005, Bolt appeared on a Melbourne breakfast radio program criticising Rayson's new play for 'accusing the navy of deliberately turning its back on drowning people at sea', and labelling her a 'cheerleader for the new barbarians' (Bolt 2005a). This was followed the next day by an article written by Bolt for his regular opinion column for the *Herald Sun*. Entitled 'Shameful saga of hate', Bolt begins by describing the play as a 'vomit of smug hate' and then writes: 'If you still need proof of how far up its own fundament our artists have crawled, go to tonight's premiere of Hannie Rayson's play ... see how cruelly and hysterically she smears our defence personnel, and anyone who even votes Liberal. God, to think such stuff passes now for art ...' (Bolt 2005b). The article attacks the play on a number of fronts; it is concerned about what Bolt sees as the play's 'hysterical' and damning version of historical events, and disputes the play's status as 'art', seeing it instead as providing a platform for the author to expound her 'vile conspiracy theory'.

Two days later, Bolt wrote again and further reinforced these views. Entitled 'Hannie's evil brew', Bolt describes Rayson as an 'activist writer' and 'a taxpayer nursed artist in this grants-stuffed culture' (Bolt 2005c). At work in this article are numerous rhetorical devices which offer a critique of the relationship between the artist and the state. Bolt constructs a picture of Rayson (and by implication all grants-reliant artists) as mendicant and narrow-minded. Bolt writes:

> I suspect it's that flood of government gold that allows Rayson to drink and drink, without having to ask nicely for water from the passing crowd instead. That great gush of public money that makes our guzzling artists praise the Lord for big government of the Left and fear the Liberal demons who might turn off the tap, and point them to their public (Bolt 2005c).

Bolt creates a sense of the unquenchable thirst of the artist drinking up the reserves of public money. In his view popular appeal is the only basis upon which the arts should be allowed to thrive. But his strongest condemnation is of artists who, like Rayson, are the beneficiaries of government largesse but use their art to criticise it. According to Bolt, Rayson is one of 'the hate-filled barbarians (sic) artists of the Left' and 'a member of the subsidised cultural elite' (Bolt 2005c).

Bolt's article attempts to produce a dichotomy between Rayson (who stands for the artist) and himself and his imagined readers (signifying the rest of society). Rayson is an uncivilised and self-indulgent force, and the reader is the unwitting taxpayer forced to foot the bill. This dichotomy is borne out in Bolt's opening line where he writes that 'It took a hot spa-full of your money to produce Hannie Rayson' (Bolt 2005c). The hot spa – with its connotations of indulgence and leisure – is set against the reference to 'your money' with its rhetorical implications that 'you' (and therefore he) are defined by hard work and self denial. Bolt reinforces the rhetoric of 'us' and 'them' throughout his article; typifying 'them' as the self-serving artists, and 'us' as the long-suffering taxpayer.

It is now a familiar rhetorical strategy in Australian public discourse whereby opposition to so-called elites (them) is established through the claim to speak for ordinary people (us) (Sawer and Hindess 2004:2). Bolt goes on to list the ways in which Rayson's career as a writer has been supported by the taxpayer because he wants the reader to see 'for yourself how government cash has trained, paid, feted, nursed and staged Rayson or her works ...' In this list Bolt mentions Rayson's training at the VCA, the staging of her plays by Australian theatre companies, her winning of a number of literary awards, her appearances at literary conferences, and the funding of her writing through government grants: all as evidence of her dependence on the largesse of the state (Bolt 2005c). It exemplifies Sawer's argument that, for neo-liberalists, the welfare state and social liberalism are often equated with female values, the 'overprotection by the state in the public sphere' making it 'incompatible with self-reliant masculinity' (2004:102). Bolt's article manifests these rhetorical features with his repeated references to Rayson's career being 'nursed' by the state, and by his insistent evocation of Rayson, in particular, and artists, in general, as dependent and mendicant.

The most explicit feature of Bolt's critique is the way he targets Rayson herself as the problem. The title of his second attack in the *Herald Sun*, 'Hannie's evil brew' illustrates this. This title explicitly identifies the writer by name; and it suggests that she is, metaphorically, poisoning the public. Bolt goes on to provide details of her career and her personal life, including the fact that she is married to academic historian Michael Cathcart who, Bolt tells us, is also the beneficiary of taxpayer-funded institutions (Bolt 2005c). This detailing of Rayson's private and professional life is proffered by Bolt to demonstrate the degree of her indebtedness to the state. It works, rhetorically, to justify the reader as a sceptic when it comes to assessing the 'value' of her work and, indeed, all state-supported arts which express a dissenting view. By explicitly targeting Rayson in this way, Bolt aims to marginalise her; she is external to the citizenry, a social outsider who is concocting treacherous deceits. Rayson and her plays are ideologically reconstructed; in Bolt's treatment she is no longer an artist creating works of fiction which legitimately promote social debate; instead she is singled out and labelled, like a witch, as an enemy of society.

Without doubt, this play and its production in Melbourne and Sydney in mid-2005 caused an unprecedented level of public discussion and debate. Simon Phillips, the play's director and the Artistic Director of the MTC, wrote 'When did you last see a play occupy the opinion columns, elicit letters of support and detraction to the editors and incur the wrath of columnists?' (Phillips 2005). While the furore around the play was remarkable for the extent of the coverage it received in the press, Andrew Bolt's response is particularly interesting for the purposes of this book. Bolt accuses Rayson of hypocrisy, selfishness and self indulgence because her play was critical of government policy. Rayson is prepared to accept government grants and live off the taxpayers' largesse, says Bolt, but refuses to concede that the majority of taxpayers voted for, and approve of, the very government policies she attacks. In this view Rayson, having received government support, should somehow acknowledge her 'obligation' through her art. Bolt is expressing the fundamental ideological perspective of neo-liberalist discourse on citizenship: citizens have duties and mutual obligations rather than 'rights'; a 'culture of dependency' is to be avoided at all costs; and self-restraint, independence from government, consumer choice and user-pays are key qualities in the development of new social capacities of citizens (Sawer and Hindess 2004).

Bolt is not responsible for formulating and implementing government policy but his response to this play suggests that he sees a role for himself in policing the ideological parameters of the culture wars. His rhetoric throughout his critique sends an unequivocal message to the reader about the proper role of the artist. In making his argument, Bolt justifies David Throsby's concern, expressed in his monograph *Does Australia Need A Cultural Policy?* (2006), that the hegemonic view of culture is not one that encourages social criticism. Instead, in the current environment artists are discouraged from 'biting the hand that feeds' while simultaneously (to change the metaphor) encouraged to relinquish the public teat. According to this view, the market will decide the merit or otherwise of artistic endeavour and it is this economic instrumentalist view that shapes much of the current cultural policy environment. Whatever judgement might be made about either the aesthetic qualities or political efficacy of Rayson's play, Bolt's response to it sends a signal that the larger project of political theatre writing in Australia, funded by government patronage, might well be an endangered activity.

Catherine McClements as Beth and Kim Gyngell as Franklin in the 2006 Company B production of *It Just Stopped*. (Photo: Heidrun Löhr)

CHAPTER 6

THE WAR ON TERROR

'Theatre as emblem of a civilised society, that's kind of what it
is' **Stephen Sewell** (2003a).

Stephen Sewell describes the current environment as 'a kind of assault
on the cultural – the way culture has been turned into entertainment'.
He argues that 'to even want to talk about theatre ... marks you as an
enemy of the state. And I think that's a valuable ... position to start
occupying and reclaiming' (Sewell 2003a). His play *Myth, Propaganda
and Disaster in Nazi Germany and Contemporary America* (2003b),
and the other plays discussed in this chapter, examine the inherent
value of free debate and the expression of politically challenging views.
For Sewell, the theatre is an important medium because: 'it's one of
the few areas that are unsupervised in this country, where you can
actually say something' (Sewell 2003a). This notion of the theatre
as 'unsupervised', and of the dramatist's duty to present politically
challenging ideas, recalls Said's suggestion, outlined in the introduction,
that intellectuals should find platforms for public address which are
relatively unencumbered by powerful interests.

The political reading provided by the plays discussed in this chapter
involves revealing the ideological frameworks which define our systems
of belief. Terry Eagleton describes ideology as 'one way among many of
accounting for the way in which what we believe is related to what we
do ...' (1997:37). And John Birmingham points out that the ideological
function of national myths manifests itself in the political arena where
the mobilising of mass opinion has become the dominant concern. To
this end, politicians, of all political hues, gain or lose support based on
'their ability to manipulate the myth and symbol of political life ...

these myths … are largely unquestioned beliefs, held by large numbers of people, which give complex and bewildering events a reassuring meaning' (Birmingham 2005:24).

The playwrights discussed here who take up this terrain lay bare the contradictions inherent in nationalist myths which appear to provide coherent explanatory frameworks for our values and beliefs. In his play *Myth, Propaganda and Disaster* Sewell begins with a monologue in the form of a history lecture given by the play's protagonist Talbot Finch. Talbot's lecture underlines the disjuncture between the apparent rationality of Nazism in its approach to the 'final solution', and the irrationality and madness of the fundamentalism that underpinned its policies. It is this contradiction between the mythologies of nationhood and the *realpolitik* of people's lives that these plays realise through the drama. The playwrights discussed here want to challenge prevailing orthodoxies and, through their dramas, challenge audiences to question taken-for-granted ideas about Australia and the people who live here. This is not a simple task. David McKnight has argued that while it is true that 'the power of ideas to shape societies is profound', it is also the case that 'we remain largely unaware of their effects in our day-to-day lives' (McKnight 2005:49). These plays make a concerted attempt to tease out this relationship between 'the power of ideas' and their impact on lived experience.

This chapter looks at a group of plays informed by the events of September 11, 2001 which interrogate how the world has been changed by terrorism and the climate of fear produced by the 'war on terror'. In particular, the focus is on two recent plays by Stephen Sewell: *It Just Stopped* (2007) and *Myth, Propaganda and Disaster in Nazi Germany and Contemporary America* (2003b).

It Just Stopped

In this 2006 play, Sewell paints a picture of society in melt down; a disaster that may have been caused by terrorism or an environmental calamity has struck and the repercussions are frightening. Performed at Melbourne's Malthouse Theatre and Belvoir St Theatre in Sydney in 2006 the production, directed by Neil Armfield, throws into relief the satirical and surreal elements of Sewell's story by placing the action in the cool normalcy of a stylish high rise apartment. The apartment's inhabitants are Beth and Franklin: a well-heeled American couple with refined tastes. Franklin is a musicologist writing an essay on Wagner for the *New York Review of Books*. Franklin's work is 'an original thesis on the cultural and psychological roots of the *nibelung*' which seeks to prove that Wagner was not an anti-Semite. With his tongue planted in his cheek Sewell has Franklin rationalising: 'well, I know he was *personally*, but I mean ... he was not anti-Semitic *musically*'. Beth is a radio producer for a shock jock broadcaster – 'Smokin' Jonesy' the 'talkback king of hate' who tells his listeners that: 'Moslems should be force-fed beer and meat pies before we let them into the place'. At first glance the couple seem to have diametrically opposed interests: Beth's patch is popular culture and Franklin is a master of arcane intellectual topics. But it is their inherent conservatism that Sewell has firmly in his sights; both Franklin and Beth can rationalise what they do in high flown theoretical terms but are utterly unprepared to grapple with the realities of people's lives, or to see the consequences of their actions in *political* terms.

Beth and Franklin's day begins like any other but soon comes off the rails as one thing after another fails to work: the computer crashes, the elevator is not working, the power goes off. They are stuck inside their beautiful apartment. At first they rationally discuss the possible causes of a power failure, but the hysteria soon mounts as it dawns of them that there may have been a cataclysmic event. They fear being cut off from the world but at the same time are terrified of engaging with it. In fact they are too scared to leave the apartment to find out what is going on. Beth cannot take the logical step of heading down the stairs: 'what if there's someone there? Hiding in the dark, waiting for me?' Fear is all-consuming and paralysing. At the same time they manifest a fear of connecting with anyone else. When Franklin suggests they check in with their neighbours, Beth seems surprised by the very idea that they *have* neighbours. She resists the suggestion that she knock on a neighbour's door as 'they've got lives of their own and what'll they think if we come around asking them what to do ...' It is a portrait of people without any semblance of community, indeed fear exacerbates their furious individualism and insularity.

Franklin insists that being 'civilised' means they are somehow inoculated against calamity: 'Beth, we've got an annual subscription to the theatre, we're not frightened of the stairs'. He is of the view that great art is somehow pristine, in its 'own sphere', and untouched by the 'grubby world of politics'. This is a theme Sewell also takes up and attacks in his play *Myth, Propaganda and Disaster* (discussed below): the idea that there is refuge to be found in the apparently pure and unsullied realm of art. Franklin insists that 'art is a higher calling. It draws us out of ourselves and ... challenges us to be better than who we are'. He repudiates the idea that art should be politically provocative as 'we don't want our artists to be lecturing us about what's wrong with the world. We want to be transported to another world'. For Sewell, this is a risible and morally reprehensible point of view. Art has to be judged not simply on aesthetic grounds but in terms of what it says and how it interacts with the world. Sewell sees art, both his own work and other people's, as an integral player in the political world; defined by and implicated in the 'grubby' political environment within which it is produced and consumed.

So focused are Beth and Franklin – him with high art and her with popular culture – that neither of them are aware of the world, and they are only dimly conscious of matters of global politics. They are not even sure if there's a war going on because 'current affairs is so depressing'. While they both claim to have special knowledge of what's *really* important, neither of them have any political awareness nor any capacity for critical self reflection. And so with disbelief they cry: 'Why me? Why us? Why would anyone want to attack us?' It is a cry which echoes the public outpouring of disbelief that Americans expressed after the events of September 11; disbelief and astonishment that the USA was not in fact loved and admired by the rest of the world.

Just as they start to panic about their circumstances another couple enters the apartment. Bill and Pearl are Australian – he is a wealthy self-made entrepreneur in the cardboard box business. The Australians make it clear that they find the American couple effete and in a state of ludicrous self-denial about the seriousness of the calamity. The American couple, on the other hand, cannot abide the crassness of the Australians who they find 'disgusting ... terrible people with awful manners and we just wish you'd go'. Bill announces that they have come to make Beth and Franklin a business proposal: 'We want you to be our slaves'. In the second half of the play the style of the work shifts between naturalistic dialogue as the two couples argue over their competing survival strategies in the brave new post-holocaust world, and more surrealistic moments which tell us that Franklin's view on things is gradually sliding into the hallucinogenic.

Sewell's play takes up a number of political themes. He addresses the wilful blindness of the middle class – people who claim to be in the know, to have their fingers on the pulse, but who are actually determinedly closed-off to political realities. Franklin says: 'We don't want to hear these terrible things – I know they're happening to someone, somewhere else – in Africa or South America, but they're not happening to me and I don't want to know about it'. Sewell suggests that such wilful closed-mindedness is all the more shocking because Beth and Franklin are people who influence debate and therefore wield cultural power. Through his writing, Franklin contributes to intellectual discourse, and through the radio program Beth helps to shape the public agenda. They are, in other words, people who use their influential cultural positions to perpetuate self-concern and rampant individualism. Sewell targets the abrogation of the social, political and environmental responsibilities of the prosperous middle class. Bill makes this abundantly clear:

> Human beings are too mad, too fucked, too selfish to do anything other than look after their most immediate interests, and if those immediate interest mean goodbye Amazon to pay for the kid's boarding school in Pennsylvania, then goodbye Amazon.

The play also strikes a distinctly anti-American note. Beth and Franklin have a sense of superiority and entitlement which, Sewell suggests, is emblematic of America's attitude to the rest of the world. Sewell articulates his critique through the character of Bill who does not pull his punches in his excoriation of America:

> You are the pornographers of the world, the polluters, the gun runners and arms salesmen of the world with more weapons of mass destruction than Saddam Hussein has had tabbouli sandwiches, and what the rest of us want to know is when the hell are you all going to stop pissing around and just grow up!

Sewell simultaneously subjects Australians to critical scrutiny. At one level Bill and Pearl are immediately familiar as Australian archetypes: Bill, in particular, is recognisably laconic and has a 'no-bullshit' approach to the world. And calling a spade a spade, we feel, is a welcome relief here where the Americans appear to be in deep denial about the hole they have dug for themselves. But there is also something ominous about Bill. He is a powerful figure, a successful entrepreneur who is used to having things go his way. His 'business proposal', that the American couple become his slaves, is unexpected and provides the point in the play from which everything takes a decidedly absurdist turn. But for all this playfulness in the writing, Sewell is careful to make it clear that these Australians are not fools or innocents. Bill is knowing and cynical, and he understands the nature of power. In this vision, contemporary Australia is not America's little deputy sheriff, but a ruthless player in a power game.

Bill understands the world because he operates in it; he is a tough and uncompromising realist who, as Sewell sees it, will therefore inherit the earth (what's left of it). It is not a joyful prospect. While Sewell is clearly contemptuous of the weakness and political irresponsibility of the educated middle classes, he is also wary of the kind of rat cunning which Bill evinces.

The play shares some telling characteristics with another recent play – Ian Wilding's *October* (2007). Wilding's play, like Sewell's, focuses on the lives (and fears) of a middle-class couple. Produced at Griffin Theatre in Sydney in 2007, the play is told in eight scenes and centres around four characters. It is set in the well-presented middle-class home of Tim and Angela. They earn a lot of money and have refined tastes, but their sheltered life is shattered when Dez enters their home and presumes a familiarity with them which they find repugnant. He insinuates that he and Angela are former lovers but she denies this and Tim insists Dez leaves.

Because Dez's intrusion brings on a surge of anxiety that neither Tim nor Angela feel they can manage, they hire an aggressive private investigator, Dick. Dick's job initially is to provide Tim and Angela with information about their intruder, to spy on him. However, Dick eggs them on to greater heights of paranoia and, fearing the possibility of further intrusions, they soon seek a more fail-safe solution – to get rid of Dez permanently. Like Sewell, Wilding is interested in the nature of fear as it seeps into the lives of the middle class. Tim and Angela are terrified by the breach of security; they see Dez's intrusion as proof of the power of the lurking, vengeful enemy who is seeking to strip away what they have worked so hard for. In their eyes the invader is a powerful figure who is not only envious and resentful, but also insidious and capable of inveigling himself right into the sacrosanct heart of the middle-class home.

In seeking to revenge themselves on this unwanted intrusion, they tell each other that their motives and methods are rational and reasonable. They maintain a discourse of self help and mouth liberal platitudes. Angela is anxious, for example, to make it clear that: 'we don't make judgements based on religion'. Tim and Angela, much like Beth and Franklin in It Just Stopped, want to project an image of themselves as 'civilised', but it is a very thin veneer. They are in fact vain, spoiled and vengeful. And like Beth and Franklin, Tim and Angela resist any idea of critical self-reflection even though, Wilding implies, it is likely that they have brought this scenario upon themselves. They ostensibly hire Dick because they fear being corrupted or exposed by the intruder, but Wilding suggests they are already corrupted. Tim, in particular, fears being unmanned by the intrusion of Dez into his house, and he reacts to this with unbridled savagery. And the character of Dick, at first a parody of the private investigator, becomes much more sinister as the play progresses. Dick promises to make Tim and Angela feel secure once again, but in fact his methods and presence in their lives becomes an uncontrollable force; violent, menacing and self-interested.

In this play, Wilding sets up the middle-class couple as a symbolic representation of the nation as it deals with the fear of invasion. The anxiety felt by Tim and Angela and their sense of vulnerability in the face of an apparent threat from inside their own home, acts as a metaphor for the fear of invasion felt by the nation after the events of September 11. It is a defensive state of being which Ghassan Hage identifies as the 'institutionalisation of a culture of worrying' (2003:3). Nikos Papastergiadis uses a psychoanalytic model to talk about the invasion complex in Australia as a 'psychic struggle to preserve an idealised self' while deploying 'mechanisms for resisting the incursion of foreign elements' (2004:11). This is reflected in the portrait constructed by Wilding; Tim and Angela strive to keep their sense of themselves as superior and in control, and their home and lifestyle sacred. Dez is the enemy who violates the boundary and must therefore be punished. This depiction reflects on the state of the nation in the grip of a phobia about the possibility of invasion, a phobia, Wilding suggests, that produces a desire for security against contamination by the outsider. Like Sewell, Wilding is interested in how the need for security is produced, and how it then rationalises its own existence so that while appearing to protect against the enemy it actually produces a heightened state of fear – and so in a self-perpetuating cycle.

Sewell and Wilding share a concern with understanding how fear is disseminated. The characters of Bill in *It Just Stopped* and Dick in *October* fulfill similar roles: they are bullies who relish in, and excel at, the production and dissemination of fear. For these writers, this is the legacy of September 11; Western societies have been brought to their knees through fear, and fearful societies are vulnerable ones. In these plays we witness a social Darwinist game as one group battles it out with another for supremacy using the sort of coercive, bully-boy tactics that makes the triumph of the powerful over the weak seem rational and inevitable.

In both plays the post-September 11 political environment is subjected to an analysis which reveals the ideological function of the social production of fear, and its corollary, enhanced state power. Sewell's interest in the power of the state is the central theme of his play *Myth, Propaganda and Disaster*. In this play, Sewell seeks to explore the relationship between state power and the suppression of dissent as a signal feature of the post-September 11 environment.

Guy Rundle argues that the suppression of dissenting discourse has been a significant strategic response by the right-wing governments in the West – and particularly in the USA and Australia – since the attack on the World Trade Centre in 2001. He describes this political strategy as the 'pathogen argument' which is systematically used by governments against those who oppose it or who express dissenting views. As he puts it, 'those critical of the unilateral American "war on terror" are not simply holders of a differing opinion within the pluralist public sphere, but are actually elements external to the citizenry: a fifth column of traitors who can be regarded as enemies of society; a disease threatening the body politic' (Rundle 2004:40).

Myth, Propaganda and Disaster in Nazi Germany and Contemporary America

> I had an interview with Julie Copeland [Radio National Arts Program] the other day and she said: 'it's very hard to shock people'. But it's easy to shock people by saying the ruling class is destroying this country and oppressing you. Try saying that somewhere and see how shocked people are (Sewell 2003a).

In his play *Myth, Propaganda and Disaster in Nazi Germany and Contemporary America*, Sewell explores the idea of dissent as pathogen and examines the way the Right exercises power. In particular, it investigates the kinds of ideological arguments used by the Right to maintain its dominance. Rundle has argued that since the attack on the World Trade Centre 'the ideology of social conservatism' has been responsible for the transformation of social debate into 'opportunities for labelling individuals and groups as enemies of society' (Rundle 2004:41). To some extent this labelling is what Hannie Rayson experienced at the hands of Andrew Bolt, as discussed in the previous chapter. Sewell's play also illustrates how labelling takes place and attempts to deconstruct the process by which liberalism has come to be regarded as a threat to Western democracies. It explores ways of understanding the politics of the Right by investigating the gradual erosion of the right to dissent whereby those who find the courage to speak with an oppositional voice are not apparently active participants in the democratic process, but traitors and enemies of the state.

Myth, Propaganda and Disaster was directed by Aubrey Mellor in Adelaide and Melbourne and by Chris Hurrell in Sydney in 2003. A further production took place in London in 2004. While the play is set in America, and explores the contemporary political landscape there, it has resonances for Australia and can be seen to participate in a broader discussion of national themes. The play has some explicit

'Australian' content (the protagonist is an expatriate Australian) and provides a parallel reading of the political processes at work in both contemporary Australian and American life.

Set soon after the events of September 11, the play focuses on university lecturer Talbot Finch, an Australian now living in the States, and teaching in the Politics Department of a prestigious American university. His American wife, Eve, is a television writer who, despite her growing professional success, feels personally unfulfilled and longs to have a child. Talbot is writing a book which traces parallels between contemporary America and Nazi Germany; in particular the systematic promulgation of fear and blame within the society in order to shore up the power-base of the ruling party. Like all nations, Talbot argues, America is constituted of a set of national myths 'about who we are and where we're going, and those myths can blind us from the reality of what we're doing and impel us toward our own destruction' (2003b:7). Many of Talbot's students, his colleagues and friends are outraged at this line of argument, believing instead that the American 'War on Terror' is the only means of safeguarding the future of freedom and democracy. Talbot is attacked by an unknown assailant who repeatedly beats and menaces him, but Jack, his Head of Department, seems unwilling to believe him when he reports it. In fact Jack is forming the view that Talbot is unstable, and that his radicalism is not good for the 'integrity' of the Department. Manufacturing a complaint of sexual harassment from a female student, Jack marginalises Talbot at work. At the same time, Talbot fails to persuade anyone that he is continuing to be abused by the mysterious assailant who accuses Talbot of being, amongst other things, 'the worst sort of terrorist – the terrorist who kills with words' (2003b:68). Finally, Eve comprehends the trouble Talbot is in, but it is too late; he is imprisoned and tortured by agents of the state on the grounds that his views are antithetical to those of the state and that he has, through his writing and teaching, effectively sanctioned terrorism.

In the play the covert operations of the state and its active participation in the suppression of dissent are laid bare. Sewell has long been interested in writing plays which denounce the injudicious exercise of power, and he sees the arts as providing important opportunities for expressing politically oppositional views: 'I feel very strongly that we are in a critical part of our world history, and that there is … a very real threat to democracy in the US. At a time like this, I think it is absolutely crucial that all artists start to address these issues, and warn and activate to try to save our democracy' (Meehan 2003).

Sewell has set the play in the well-heeled, bourgeois environment of the American intelligentsia and the set design of Mellor's production emphasised the blank impersonal spaces in which Talbot lives and works. Throughout the drama, images such as the American flag and swastikas, projected on a large screen at the back of the stage, helped to evoke the sense of omnipresent state control and its historic link with patriotic iconography. It is post-September 11 and the sense of impending threat is everywhere; there are security scares in shopping centres in downtown Manhattan, and regular security lock downs at the university. Students must pass through Security and make appointments to see their professors – the university is an environment where contact between people is regulated by the operations of security. This works to create the impression that the institution (and therefore the state) is acting responsibly to protect those in its care but the security presence has a self-reinforcing function: it reproduces the fear of terrorism which it claims to circumvent. The members of the American intelligentsia in this play are angry and frightened by the events of September 11, but they don't seek explanations. Sewell portrays a culture which resists truth-seeking about the complex nature and origins of anti-Americanism behind the terrorist acts of September 11, and instead expresses an almost lustful desire for revenge. At the start of the play, Talbot and Eve have a dinner party with their friends and work colleagues where the subject of terrorism is discussed. Amy, Jack's wife, explains she is glad that possible terrorist suspects are being captured and tortured in Jordan, and that 'if I was there in Jordan now, I'd buy my popcorn and I'd line up to pay my ten dollars to watch' (2003b:8). In their uncritical acceptance of the state's propaganda about the 'war on terror', Sewell argues, the intelligentsia has been corrupted and co-opted.

Sewell has picked his setting carefully to demonstrate the nature and extent of the dominant view's persuasiveness. The university, after all, is a putative bastion of independent thought, and academics are engaged in the intellectual task of critical enquiry. Yet these very people are not just capitulating to, but actively promulgating, the new world order. Sewell has a dig at postmodernism when Talbot's ambitious Australian friend Max has a fashionably 'postmodern' idea for a book on the topic 'does the State exist?' – a subject area which Max expediently judges will be good 'for the CV' (2003b:31). But Sewell has something more serious in mind than satirising the faddish theoretical concerns of academics. Indeed, Sewell suggests that a depoliticising of the critical nature of intellectual enquiry has been brought about by the corporatisation of the universities, and by postmodernism's repudiation of notions of 'truth' and 'reality', a tendency which Terry Eagleton says has 'charmed the business executive' and is 'music to the ears of the advertising agency' (Eagleton 1997:28).

Sewell is also damning about the way art is appropriated in this brave new world; here art is a distraction, an entertainment, a means of papering over the cracks to provide a veneer of the apparently civilising effects of cultural appreciation. Eve is a successful television and film scriptwriter making popular American dramas, but as Talbot is increasingly convinced of the Machiavellian operations of the State, he challenges her to justify the need for 'one more Michael Douglas movie' to 'make everyone think everything is normal' (2003b:52). Talbot and his colleagues are cultured people and they go to art openings. But the function of this art is to amuse, distract and create the illusion that a fine sensibility is all that is needed for the middle class to persuade itself of its own moral superiority. Towards the end of the play Talbot's various academic colleagues and their wives gather at an art exhibition at the Guggenheim while, at the same time, Talbot himself is imprisoned and tortured for promoting terrorism by promulgating liberalist views. The inconsequential social chitchat of the academics as they move around the Guggenheim, and the revelation of their small infidelities, is cut through with the sound of Talbot's agonised screams. In this environment, Sewell seems to suggest, art which does not speak out about politics and truth is a smokescreen. It allows the bourgeoisie to see itself as 'cultured' while at the same moment they turn their backs on the suffering that is taking place right under their noses. At the end of this scene a distraught Eve bursts in; she has tracked Jack to the Guggenheim and begs him for help in finding Talbot. Jack tries to usher her out and quieten her hysteria, but she yells 'They've got my husband! They've got my goddamn husband!' (2003b:83). In a chilling closure to the scene, Eve's outburst is mistaken for a performance by gallery visitors who clap in appreciation: thus the genuine expression of terror and despair is simultaneously aestheticised and reduced to meaninglessness.

It is not just in the universities and the arts where there is evidence of a culture 'in terrible crisis'. The world that Sewell has created in this play is shaped by systematic state control producing fear, threat and violence. This promotion of fear establishes the belief in the need for security by which the end justifies the means, so establishing the preconditions for Fascism. Talbot, recalling Eisenhower's 1961 speech about the Military–Industrial Complex, argues that the 'Security State, the Intelligence State … is just under the surface waiting to break through'. Further, Talbot believes that the 'Military–Industrial Complex is using the terrorist crisis to stage a takeover' (2003b:31). The play dramatises the staging of this ideological takeover by representing Talbot as one of a dying breed whose self-proclaimed liberalism and idealism makes him a target for elimination. The 'war on terror' is a ruse for state-sanctioned action to eradicate opposition and dissent from within its own ranks thereby saving America from 'the plague of liberalism' (2003b:45).

Another recent play, *The Spook* (2005) by Melissa Reeves, takes up an interest in the covert operations of the state. Reeves' play is not literally about terrorism, nor does it directly explore the events of September 11 – indeed it is set in the mid-1960s and looks at a group of Communist Party members living in the Victorian country town of Bendigo during the Cold War. However the play's concern with government surveillance and dissent resonates with the current era and with Sewell's depiction of these issues in his play. In *The Spook* Martin, a 19-year-old Bendigo man, is conscripted by the mysterious Alex, a local ASIO (Australian Security and Intelligence Organisation) operative. Martin is told to spy on the 'little nest of reds' that regularly meet to 'bag Menzies' and discuss *Das Kapital* around the barbeque

(2005:4). Alex convinces Martin that this group of locals from the South Bendigo Branch of the Communist Party is dangerous, unpatriotic and a menace to society: 'They're zealots, and they've lost their humanity. Or at the very least they're naïve. They're Russia's finger puppets ...' (2005:28).

As the story unfolds it becomes clear, however, that the real zealot is Alex. The lack of power and influence exercised by this little regional sub-branch of the Communist Party, demoralised as it is by internal factional fighting, is palpable. Yet Alex is so determined to bring down this group of 'commies' that he invents allegations against them and plants false documents. It is a measure of how profoundly Alex is fired by Cold War propaganda and paranoia that he insists that the international disunity of the Communist Party, that was in evidence by the mid-1960s, is actually a Communist plot designed to destabilise the West with misinformation.

In his introduction to the play, historian Stuart McIntyre notes that ASIO maintained an active anti-Communist operation throughout the 1960s and engaged in 'following Communist Party members, intercepting communications, tapping phones, bugging meeting places, blacklisting members from employment' (Reeves 2005:viii). Like Sewell, Reeves sees such forms of government surveillance, rationalised by heightened patriotic fervour, as an insidious means of exercising hegemonic power. She notes that such activities are not simply an historical phenomenon associated with Cold War politics:

> In our era with its 'war on terror', demonisation of Muslims, and a heightened criticism, even censorship of any dissenting view, our security organisations and the governments that unleash them are again exercising great power over people's lives (Reeves Program Notes 2007).

McIntyre notes similar parallels between the Cold War and contemporary politics when he describes the 'distorting prism of surveillance'. In her portrayal of Cold War thinking as a clash of values Reeves also helps to evoke contemporary politics. Dennis Altman has pointed out that most of the current crop of politicians grew up with such Cold War thinking and have now transposed it to the current time so that: 'the world is divided between the forces of good, namely the

West, and a motley collection of rogue states, fundamental Islamists and terrorists who together attack democracy and "our way of life" (Altman 2007).

A further parallel that might be drawn between the two eras is in the play's portrayal of the notion of the enemy within. With Alex's urging, Martin believes that society is being undermined by a hidden, internal enemy. This aspect of Cold War thinking (neatly encapsulated by the notion of 'Reds under the Beds') promulgated the view that Australian Communist Party members were surreptitiously inveigling their way into positions of power in order to undermine the state. Alex tells Martin:

> You know how many commie teachers there are out there, Martin, thousands, it's a policy they've got, it's written in their fucking constitution, infiltrate the schools, across the board … breed a whole generation of people that think like them, and look how well it's worked, look at the fucking students, pissing on the cops, sitting in the middle of the fucking road … (2005:29–30).

This interest in the notion of the enemy within is one that Reeves shares with Sewell in *Myth, Propaganda and Disaster*. The argument that the state needs increased powers to protect its citizens is harnessed to this notion that an insidious enemy lurks within a community, seeking opportunities to undermine it. *The Spook* is a provocative account of how ASIO, as an agent of state power in the 1960s, promulgated a sense of fear about the infiltration of communists into the community which, in turn, provided an ends to justify whatever means they chose to adopt. Sewell portrays the discourses around the 'war on terror' in the current political environment in much the same way. It provokes community fear and suspicion, thereby providing a rationale for intensifying state power to protect the community. Underlining this point, the program notes of the Melbourne production of *The Spook* quote UK playwright Harold Pinter: 'Herman Goering once said that all you have to do to retain power is to tell the people that you are protecting them' (Reeves Program Notes 2007).

Reeves' play is set in Australia and explicitly reflects on aspects of Australian political history. In contrast, *Myth, Propaganda and Disaster* is set in contemporary America to expose the founding national myths which appear to provide plausible definitions of the nation. The myth of democracy, he suggests, underpinned by the unshakeable belief in the value of individualism, lies at the heart of American self-definition. The state uses this 'story' of nationhood in order to shore up its power base; America is in the business, Sewell argues, of protecting democracy through a strategy of identifying and persecuting convenient enemies. Thus the state expediently manipulates the notion of democracy to its own political advantage. Michael Billington, London theatre reviewer for the *Guardian*, noted Sewell's portrait of contemporary America as a 'country in which the Socratic quest for truth is subordinate to iron certainty' (Billington 2004). In this middle-class milieu, people seem content with their certainties and only too willing to ignore the contradictions inherent in the democratic myth, as Talbot says: 'We are torturing people in Jordan, but sitting here in New York watching *Seinfeld* and imagining ourselves to be the guardians of freedom and democracy in the world' (2003b:7). Sewell suggests that it takes a consensual delusion to continue to insist that American democracy is liberating the world. While Talbot retains a wilful idealism and insists that democracy must still mean something, his brilliant young student, the determinedly radical Margurite Lee, argues differently, that no one any longer believes that America is a democracy. The radicalised young, she argues, are more cynical and knowing: 'What people want to know is how power is being manipulated, and by whom and what they can do about it' (2003b:13). Her sharp and pragmatic view of the world, however, is no more protection for her than Talbot's idealism is for him; she too ends up a casualty of the war on dissent. Both are enemies of society finally eliminated by the state in its paradoxical role as the protector of democracy. Sewell clearly dramatises the relationship, identified by Rundle, between coercive state control and the social production of 'fear, dependency and victimisation' (Rundle 2004:59).

While the play is explicitly focused on America, the concern to deconstruct national mythologies makes the play relevant to this discussion of politically challenging writing for the Australian stage. Indeed, Sewell gives many of his plays an international setting which acts as a crucible for his critique of Australian politics. *It Just Stopped* continues and develops this practice by deliberately fudging the play's location so that, at various times, the audience thinks they might be in New York or Melbourne. In *Myth, Propaganda and Disaster* the enmeshing of Australian and American political identities is a part of Sewell's critical deconstruction of Australian nationalism. Here Australian national mythologies of independence, egalitarianism, anti-authoritarianism, an inherently democratic instinct – are all found wanting. Instead Australia is seen as an active participant in the production and maintenance of the existing relations of power. The Australian expatriate academic Max is sycophantic towards America. He thinks Talbot has it all: 'an American wife, residency, a teaching post at a prestigious university'; and he can't understand why Talbot would make trouble. Max is of the view that Australia is 'finished'; 'it's just one big joke', but America is 'real', he says, because it is powerful; 'when America says something, people listen' (2003b:10). This is a portrait of the new Australian, attracted by power; greedy, opportunistic and sycophantic, the outsider who longs for credibility with the insiders. Max's lecture in the play's closing moments is chilling. He has 'replaced' Talbot – both literally and metaphorically. Max tows the American imperialist line and his statements reflect the current pro-American alliance fostered by the Howard Government. As one critic noted: 'Max's immersive metamorphosis into a true-blue Stars and Stripes toady appears to be Sewell's metaphoric portrait of Australia's current relationship with the United States' (Low 2003). There is no place in Max's world view for dissent or critique, but rather an uncritical employment of the rhetoric of good and evil. His speech at the play's close represents the total capitulation of the intelligentsia to the hegemonic power of the state. It represents Australia's willing collusion in the manufacture of totalising mythologies which mask the state's ideological agendas. And we end with a picture of the unshakeable self righteousness and awesome power of a ruling body which, while claiming to have secured the triumph of freedom and democracy, will not itself tolerate opposition.

Some critical responses to the play pointed to its timeliness and political punch. Low, for example, described the Sydney production as: 'a blast of fresh theatrical air in a cultural and political climate starving for it' (Low 2003). On the other hand, some reviewers felt the play lapsed into polemic and melodrama. Reviewing for the *Australian*, On described the play as suffering from 'a bloated, self-conscious wordiness ... the violence becomes gratuitous and the narrative becomes literally and metaphorically heavy-handed, with the tension and tautness of earlier interactions undermined by the melodrama of the interrogation scenes' (On 2003b).

The criticism levelled at *Myth, Propaganda and Disaster* reveals the tensions that can exist between drama and polemic in some political theatre. This issue was highlighted by the arts and cultural commentator Peter Craven who has discussed the particular difficulties of writing political theatre. He makes the point that while politics does not make an impossible partner to theatre (as playwrights such as Bertolt Brecht, Jean-Paul Sartre and Arthur Miller testify), it is nonetheless a difficult relationship (2005:16). Craven says the mark of great political theatre is manifested in the dramatist's capacity to 'represent points of view that are not sympathetic to the author' (2005:16). Craven goes on to provide a critique of Rayson's play *Two Brothers* (2005) and David Williamson's play *Influence* (2005) on the basis that neither of these managed the necessary 'dialectical engagement' (2005:16). The key here, he argues, is not that the dramatist must endorse views that he/she finds politically repellent but 'they must have the formal sympathy that allows the dramatic figure to burn themselves into significance on the stage' (2005:16).

Terry Eagleton counters this view when he questions the liberal myth of 'judicious even-handedness' (2003:136). He is not referring specifically to political theatre; however his point offers a retort to Craven's call for a more even-handed approach to dramatic representation. Eagleton notes that there are situations – 'all the key political situations' – in which 'one side has a good deal more of the truth than the other' (2003:136). Even-handedness, says Eagleton, is not always 'in the service of objectivity' (2003:137). Eagleton, then, sees value in the passionate stance and in taking up a position since 'you can only know how the situation is if you are in a *position* to know. Only by standing at a certain angle to reality can it be illuminated for you' (2003:135). A good example of the passionate stance comes from Stephen Sewell who does not see his task as one of representing alternative points of view in the way that Craven advocates. Rather, Sewell's political theatre practice emerges out of his concern to speak with passion (if not anger), using his prosodic facility to illuminate reality from his point of view. All the writers discussed in this book are juggling the demands of the craft with their own political passions – a most difficult balancing act. Sharing an abiding interest in writing about the political sphere, their work evinces a characteristic dialectical negotiation with truth and objectivity.

In an interview Sewell reveals a nuanced reading of this dilemma for the writer. He argues that Australian theatre writers, as a rule, avoid the political matters of the day; 'we are not doing what we need to do – we are not saying the hard things that we need to say, we are not insisting that we have the right to say them' (Sewell 2003a). Further, he notes the qualities writers need to enable them to say the 'hard things':

> I use every opportunity I can when I'm talking to writers to say ... it's finding the key to your own soul and having the courage or stupidity to open those doors ... you need that audacity and that madness and when you ... embrace that ... that is when you begin to give the audience what they want, and need. They want to be taken by the hand and led into their own heart (Sewell 2003a).

The writers discussed in this chapter, Stephen Sewell, Ian Wilding and Melissa Reeves have written audacious plays, and they have written courageously. This group of plays is concerned to unravel and reveal the nature of state power and the recent triumph of fear as an outcome of state-sanctioned control measures. These are plays which reveal an ideological understanding of the social production of fear and the concomitant production of the need for greater security measures. We learn that, paradoxically, the discourses of democratic freedom have been co-opted to rationalise increased state control. It is, after all, the work of ideology to construct a unified face to the paradoxical and contradictory tensions that make up our understanding of the world we live in. It is the work of this group of plays to understand the ideological underpinnings of our beliefs and values, and to ask questions about how we have come to be where we are, and believe what we do.

Kellie Higgins as Sally, Peter Barry as Phil and Emma Wood as Tania in the 2005 New
Theatre Production of *Falling Petals*. (Photo: Phil Sheather)

Conclusion

In *The Playwright as Thinker*, Eric Bentley makes a telling point about how important it is for the work of the playwright to be apprehended in the time and place in which it was written. Once we discard the assumption of art's timelessness, he says, we can then appreciate that:

> ... historical interpretation is not merely an apparatus to help fill out the details of our understanding of Shakespeare and Ibsen; we shall find that Shakespeare's individuality lies in his Elizabethanness and not in his timelessness ... The arts are fragments of the time and place which produced them and cannot be comprehended either conceptually or imaginatively, outwardly or inwardly, without a knowledge and imaginative understanding of their context (Bentley 1974:56).

Derrida (1976) makes the opposite point in his demonstration of how the classicist does not use Homer's 'Greekness' in order to comprehend imaginatively *The Odyssey*. Indeed, *The Odyssey* is scrutinised by classicists to get a grip on end-of-Dark-Age 'Greekness' as was anticipated by Moses Finley in 1954 (Finley 1954). But this book is author-based; a study of what a group of playwrights have to say about themselves. The classicists lack authors to speak to, whereas I can interrogate mine. Using the writers' views of their vocation, together with an analysis of their work, I have sought, echoing Bentley, to understand the relationship of contemporary Australian playwriting to the political circumstances and the cultural background in which it emerged. I am not making claims as to the timeless or universal qualities of the plays of Rayson or Sewell or Cribb. Rather the opposite is true: I have attempted to show that what is interesting and important about the work of the playwrights I discuss is its *contemporary Australianness*;

its commitment to the investigation of the here and the now.

Peter Craven takes a different view when discussing the perennially controversial Miles Franklin Award for Australian literature. He argues that the history of the Miles Franklin Award reveals an obsession with Australianness and this in turn bespeaks a certain parochialism and cultural insecurity, as if our longing to see ourselves embodied through artistic representation might 'confirm our right to cultural existence' (Craven 2007). Craven insists that 'the imagination cannot be tethered by nationalism' and he is, of course, right. There are many recent Australian plays, for example, which are imaginative and powerful but which are not concerned with nationalism and politics. And this does not diminish their achievement. But I have chosen to highlight those plays which tell us about where we live; and the nationalist subject matter of such drama and fiction, as Craven points out, 'doesn't make them better, it simply makes them ours' (Craven 2007). I have not made the claim that the plays discussed in this book are better than other plays, just that they are doing something culturally significant by being explicitly ours. In the current climate, I have argued, this commitment, this *doing*, is considerable and considered.

'Australianness' has always been a much-contested notion and governments have worked, with great success, at promulgating various versions of that idea. It is in this ideological terrain that contemporary Australian theatre can be found staking its claim on the national imagination. Perhaps it is more accurate to say that this is where theatre *continues* to be found since the history of Australian theatre is nothing if not a history of staging the nation. This national–cultural project has arguably been in evidence since the 1890s. But with the advent of state support for the arts in the late 1960s there has been an explicit harnessing of the nation-building rhetoric of government with the creative endeavours of Australian theatre artists. This book has argued that the current moment is marked by a new tension in that historic relationship – and it is this contextual moment which forms the backdrop for the discussion that has taken place here.

Guy Rundle has noted that in the decade from the late 1980s Australia saw 'the dimming of the radical national project' (Rundle 2006:12). The project, and its objective to capture a strong and historically located sense of national identity, was the catalyst for the production of important films like *The Chant of Jimmie Blacksmith*. The film released in 1978, was not a popular success but it was critically significant because it struck Australian audiences as a 'central expression of the culture and what concerned us' (Rundle 2006:12). As the national cultural project faltered through the 1990s, Rundle argues, artists lost their way: Australian plays and films settled for the ironic and playful, the exploration of small identities and 'not the big I' (Rundle 2006:12). But from 2001, he says, history comes 'roaring back'. A convergence of three critical incidents from the start of the new millennium put politics and history back on the arts agenda: the attack on the World Trade Centre on September 11, 2001; the anti-globalisation movement in the face of the domination of neo-liberalism; and the crisis over the detention of refugees – 'the kiss of the whip [which] turned all those who didn't do something into jailers, consenting with their silence' (Rundle 2006:13).

The writers discussed here have responded to 'the return of history' and grappled with big political questions that have emerged in its wake. In their work they have resolutely not used irony to elide political engagement. The plays discussed in this book are part of Australia's public intellectual response to international issues around globalisation, the rise of neo-liberalism, the war on terror, and the great tides of refugees seeking a place to call home. Given the scale of such global turmoil, and the various calamities that have produced or been produced by it, it should be no surprise that many Australian playwrights are fired by a sense of political purpose. As I've argued throughout, the Australian theatre has been, on important occasions, a place of public deliberation and passionate discussion of the causes and consequences of political and ideological change.

If Australia's place on the global stage has been the subject of recent drama, so too, have national issues: in particular, the ongoing fight over interpretations of history, along with the derailing of the projects of reconciliation and multiculturalism. Robert Manne has described what he sees as a 'profound transformation' in Australia – 'a kind of conservative–populist counter-revolution' – which has resulted in the abandonment of the idea of reconciliation and multiculturalism

(Manne 2007:vii). The plays I have discussed have documented this 'transformation'. They have asked the question: what does it mean for us as a nation to have turned away from the task of reconciliation and the project of multiculturalism? And they have asked this question in a range of politically provocative ways. But their goal is not simply provocation; it is to posit an alternative mode of democratic engagement, one that repudiates the xenophobia of hegemonic nationalism, and is informed by a progressive commitment to the idea of a national community.

Why is the theatre a place where such trenchant political analysis is to be found? This book begins with an account of UK playwright David Hare's lecture delivered while visiting Australia in 2004. Hare has dedicated his working life to creating political theatre and thinking about the role of theatre as a vital means for ventilating democracy. And Hare argues that the theatre's signal characteristic is its capacity to expose the difference between 'what a man says and what he does':

> A man steps forward and informs the audience of his intention
> to lifelong fidelity to his wife, while his hand, even as he speaks,
> drifts at random to the body of another woman. The most basic
> dramatic situation you can imagine; the gap between what he
> says and what we see him to be opens up, and in that gap we see
> something that makes theatre unique ... (Hare 2005:114)

This gap is where the theatre's capacity to politicise audiences is palpable. It is the work of ideology to construct a persuasive, apparently totalised and 'reassuringly pliable' view of the world (Eagleton 1997:87). As Hare describes it, it is the work of theatre to unsettle the taken-for-granted-ness of ideology by showing the gap between what is said and what is seen to be done. In this way, Hare points out, theatre has a 'unique suitability to illustrating an age in which men's ideals and men's practice bear no relation to each other' (Hare 2005:114). Such a view is shared by the playwrights discussed here who, like Andrew Bovell understand the imperative of the theatre to unsettle, and to present audiences with new ways of seeing:

> I write for theatre because I believe it's an effective medium to
> talk about difficult ideas and take a critical position in regard to
> our own culture; to create a critical framework of my culture
> (Bovell 2002a).

This book has developed from interviews with key Australian theatre practitioners and an analysis of their plays. All of these playwrights, in being asked to discuss their role and their objectives as contemporary theatre writers, seemingly revealed a paradox: on the one hand they articulated a passionate engagement with the notion of the nation and a commitment to interrogating the specificities of Australian life and politics, and on the other hand they expressed profoundly critical views on the notion of the nation as constructed and promulgated by governments. I say 'seemingly' because there is no paradox; the writers' statements about themselves and their objectives revealed that they are heterodox; they work against the grain. And in identifying their heterodoxy, I coined the term 'critical nationalism' as a way of conjuring with both the deeply critical stance of these writers and their continuing concern to keep the notion of the nation in play.

I began with a question about how a group of contemporary Australian playwrights respond, through their work, to the political environment. The plays analysed here have invited an interrogation of the idea of political theatre and this interrogation has been informed by what the writers themselves have to say about their role as contributors to public debate. The argument that critique is a primary objective of these writers is substantiated by the writers' own self-descriptions. One of the clear ways in which they understand their role is in terms of the practice of political theatre. While the writers differ in the range of forms, styles and genres they employ, they are united in their commitment to theatre as a forum for principled critical engagement in the public sphere.

A thematic reading of issues around place, race and history, and class and power in the plays evidences a strong link between their subject matters and the social, economic and political environment in which they were written and to which they respond. They can be read as a repudiation of neo-liberalism and the government rhetoric around one nation. Instead, these plays construct portraits of the nation as fundamentally divided. Here are plays which see generational, racial and class-based divisions as being primary and defining characteristics of the nation. In a political environment dominated by hegemonic nationalist discourses of 'one people, one nation', they are a significant countervailing voice.

At the same time, I have argued that these writers have not given up on the nation as an entity worth 'caring about' (to echo Ghassan Hage). The nation, its peoples, idioms and stories, continue to be evoked in these plays as meaningful and familiar constructions. And the playwrights, despite their critiques of hegemonic nationalism, are clearly prepared to 'care'.

David McKnight has discussed the importance of moving beyond the moribund ideological paradigms of Right and Left and suggests that the time is right to think about a new political outlook based on values which he calls a 'new humanism' (McKnight 2005:248). This new humanism, he argues, would entail the production of 'a moral vision of the nation' involving a 'politically progressive force which seeks mass support to project a different idea of "Australianness"' – one that defines 'the Australian way as one of equity, fairness and tolerance' (2005:257). While McKnight does not specifically mention the arts or culture as a mechanism for the production of a new moral vision, this is precisely the terrain in which these playwrights operate. They are indeed a 'progressive force' whose work is on view to large audiences in Australian mainstream theatres. They are primarily involved, as I have shown, in the circulation of ideas around 'Australianness', and they imply a moral imperative for a more equitable, fair and tolerant reading of nationhood. These writers may well help to realise McKnight's vision of a new humanism and in so doing revivify a new and timely consensus between nation and culture.

References

In the main text, the year in brackets after a play title refers to the year of its first production. Hence *Harbour* (2004) was first produced in 2004. However if an extract from a published play is quoted in the text, the reference refers to the year of publication and includes a page reference (Thomson 2005b:45).

Interviews

All interviews were conducted by the author.

Bovell, Andrew. 2002a Interview with Bovell. Melbourne.

Cornelius, Patricia. 2002 Interview with Cornelius. Melbourne.

Cribb, Reg. 2005 Interview with Cribb. Sydney.

Ellis, Ben. 2005 Interview with Ellis. Melbourne.

Enoch, Wesley. 2005 Interview with Enoch. Melbourne.

Rayson, Hannie. 2003a Interview with Rayson (1). Melbourne

Rayson, Hannie. 2005a Interview with Rayson (2). Melbourne.

Sewell, Stephen. 2003a Interview with Sewell. Melbourne.

Thomson, Katherine. 2005a Interview with Thomson. Sydney.

Select Bibliography

Albrechtson, J. 2006 'Textbook case of making our past a blame game'. *Australian*. February 1.

Altman, Dennis. 2007 'It's time to take the blinkers off'. *Age*. February 21.

Anderson, Tammy. 2002 'I Don't Wanna Play House'. *Blak Inside: 6 Indigenous Plays from Victoria*. Sydney: Currency Press.

Ang, Ien. 2003 'From White Australia to Fortress Australia: The Anxious Nation in the New Century'. *Legacies of White Australia: Race, Culture and Nation*. Eds. L. Jayasuriya, D. Walker & J. Gothard. Crawley, WA: University of Western Australia Press, 51–69.

Australian Reconciliation Convention. 1997 Indigenous Law Resources Reconciliation and Social Justice Library http://beta.austlii.edu.au/au/other/IndigLRes/

Archer, Robyn. 2005 *The Myth of the Mainstream: Politics & the Performing Arts in Australia Today*. Sydney: Currency House.

Ball, Martin. 2003 'Layered motifs bound to resonate off-stage'. *Australian*. March 10.

Bentley, Eric. 1974 *The Playwright as Thinker*. San Diego: Harcourt Brace.

Billington, Michael. 2004 'A Nazi view of America today. Myth, Propaganda and Disaster in Nazi Germany and Contemporary America'. *Guardian*. November 15:24.

Birmingham, John. 2005 `So happy we could scream – still comfortable but relaxed no more in John Howard's Australia'. *The Monthly* 1(1): 21–27.

Blainey, Geoffrey. 1984 *All for Australia*. Sydney. Methuen Haynes.

Boland, Michaela. 2004a 'Last Cab to Darwin'. *Daily Variety*. August 29.

Boland, Michaela. 2004b 'Sydney's Nevin makes a splash'. *Variety*. January 18:58.

Bolt, Andrew. 2005a 3AW Breakfast. Media Monitors. 12/4/05. *Ross Stevenson Breakfast Program*. ID M00017397908. AC Nielsen.

Bolt, Andrew. 2005b 'Shameful saga of hate'. *Herald Sun*. Melbourne. April 13.

Bolt, Andrew. 2005c 'Hannie's evil brew'. *Herald Sun*. Melbourne. April 15:23.

Bourdieu, Pierre. 1986 *Distinction: A Social Critique of the Judgment of Taste*. London: Routledge.

Bovell, Andrew. 2000 'Trash' in *Who's Afraid of the Working Class?*, *Melbourne Stories: Three Plays*. Sydney: Currency Press.

Bovell, Andrew. 2001 *Holy Day*. Sydney: Currency Press.

Bovell, Andrew. 2002b 'The Chair' in *Fever* by Bovell et. al. unpublished manuscript in the possession of HLA Management.

Bovell, Andrew. 2006 'Political Theatre: Keynote Address', (unpublished) Melbourne Writers' Festival, Malthouse Theatre, Melbourne August 27.

Bradley, L. 2000 'Choosing good ground: a forum interview with Kooemba Jdarra artistic directors Lafe Charleton, Wesley Enoch and Nadine McDonald'. *Australasian Drama Studies* (37): 59–67.

Bramwell, Murray. 2001 'Cause and effect'. *Australian*. August 24:19.

Brett, Judith. 2002 *Australian Liberals and the Moral Middle Class*. Port Melbourne: Cambridge University Press.

Brett, Judith. 2003 'John Howard and the Australian legend'. *Arena* 6(5):19–24.

Brisbane, Katharine. 1979 'Foreword'. *The Man from Muckinupin*. Dorothy Hewett. Perth, Fremantle: vii–viii.

Brisbane, Katharine. 1995 'The Future in Black and White: Aboriginality in Recent Australian Drama', Sydney: Currency Press.

Carter, David. 2004 'The Conscience Industry: The Rise and Rise of the Public Intellectual', *The Ideas Market*. Ed. D. Carter. Melbourne: Melbourne University Press 15–39

Case, Sue-Ellen. 1988 *Feminism and Theatre*. New York: Methuen.

Casey, Maryrose. 2004 *Creating Frames: Contemporary Indigenous Theatre*. St Lucia: University of Queensland Press.

Castles, Stephen., M. Kalantzis, W. Cope & M. Morrissey. 1988 *Mistaken Identity Multiculturalism and the Demise of Nationalism in Australia*. Sydney: Pluto.

Castles, Stephen. 2001 'Multiculturalism in Australia'. *The Australian People: An Encyclopedia of the Nation, Its People and Their Origins*. Ed. J. Jupp. Cambridge: Cambridge University Press.

Clark, Chelsea. 2003 'Plight of the unwanted'. *Daily Telegraph*. September 16:25.

Commonwealth of Australia. *Creative Nation*. 1994 Canberra: Commonwealth of Australia.

Cornelius, Patricia. 2000 'Money' in *Who's Afraid of the Working Class?, Melbourne Stories: Three Plays*. Sydney: Currency Press.

Cribb, Reg. 2003 *Last Cab to Darwin*. Unpublished manuscript in the possession of HLA Management.

Cribb, Reg. 2003 *The Return*. Sydney: Currency Press.

Craven, Peter. 2005 'Shadow Play'. *Weekend Australian*. June 16–18:16–17.

Craven, Peter. 2007 'Reward the best novel, not the most Australian one'. *Age*. April 23: 11.

Curran, James. 2004 *The Power of Speech: Australian Prime Ministers Defining the National Image*. Melbourne: Melbourne University Press.

Curthoys, Ann. 2000 'Mythologies'. *The Australian Legend and its Discontents*. Ed. R. Nile. St. Lucia: Queensland University Press.

Davis, Mark. 1997 *Gangland*. Sydney: Allen & Unwin.

D'Cruz, Glenn. 2005 '"Class" & Political Theatre: The case of Melbourne Workers Theatre'. *New Theatre Quarterly* 21(3):207–217.

Derrida, Jacques. 1976 *Of Grammatology*. Trans. G. Spivak. Johns Hopkins University Press.

Dodson, Michael. 2004 'Indigenous Australians'. *The Howard Years*. R. Manne. Melbourne: Black Inc.:119–143.

Dunne, Stephen. 2003a 'Social truths come home to the nest'. *Sydney Morning Herald*. July 24:17.

Dunne, Stephen. 2003b 'Opening doors on a strong sense of social self-harm'. *Sydney Morning Herald*. September 18:19.

Eagleton, Terry. 1980 'Towards a critique of political fiction'. *Meanjin* 39/3: 383–388.

Eagleton, Terry. 1997 *The Ideology of the Aesthetic*. Oxford: Blackwell.

Eagleton, Terry. 2003 *After Theory*. London: Allen Lane Penguin Books.

Ellis, Ben. 2002 *Post Felicity*. Sydney: Currency Press.

Ellis, Ben. 2003 *Falling Petals*. Sydney: Currency Press.

Ellis, Ben. 2004 *These People*. Sydney: Currency Press.

Enoch, Wesley & Mailman, Deborah. 2002 *The 7 Stages of Grieving*. Brisbane: Playlab Press.

Enoch, Wesley. 2007 *The Story of the Miracles at Cookie's Table*. Sydney: Currency Press.

Esslin, Martin. 1987 *The Theatre of the Absurd*. New York: Penguin

Esson, Louis. 1999 'The Drovers'. *Louis Esson: Plays 1. J*. Senczuk. Wollongong: Five Island Press.

Esson, Louis. 1920 'The Woman Tamer'. *Dead Timber and Other Plays*. London: Henderson.

Esson, Louis. 1973 *The Time is Not Yet Ripe*. Sydney: Currency Methuen Drama.

Fensham, Rachel & Varney, Denise. 2005 *The Doll's Revolution: Australian Theatre and the Cultural Imaginary*. Melbourne: Australian Scholarly Publishing.

Finley, Moses. 1954 *The World of Odysseus*. London: Chatto & Windus.

Fitzgerald, Michael. 2004 'Battlers take a bow'. *Time International*, 3. January 26:63.

Fitzpatrick, Peter. 1979 *After The Doll': Australian Drama Since 1955*. Melbourne: Edward Arnold.

Fitzpatrick, Peter. 1995 *Pioneer Players*. Cambridge: Cambridge University Press.

Fotheringham, Richard. 1992 'The Politics of Theatre and Political Theatre in Australia'. *The Politics of Theatre and Drama*. Ed. G. Holderness. London: Macmillan: 66–83.

Frankland, Richard. 2002 *Conversations with the Dead* in *Blak Inside: 6 Indigenous Plays from Victoria*. Sydney: Currency Press.

Furedi, Frank. 2004 *Where Have All the Intellectuals Gone?* London: Continuum.

Futcher, Michael & Howard, Helen. 2000 *A Beautiful Life*. Sydney: Currency Press.

Gibson, Lisanne. 2001 *The uses of art: constructing Australian identities*. St. Lucia: University of Queensland Press.

Gilbert, Helen. 1998a *Sightlines: Race, Gender and Nation in Contemporary Australian Theatre*. Ann Arbor: University of Michigan Press.

Gilbert, Helen. 1998b 'Reconciliation? Aboriginality and Australian Theatre'. *Our Australian Theatre in the 1990s*. Ed. V. Kelly. Amsterdam: Rodopi.

Gilbert, Helen. 2003 'Millennial Blues: racism, nationalism and the legacy of empire'. *Playing Australia: Australian Theatre and the International Stage*. Eds. E. Schafer & S. Bradley Smith. Amsterdam: Rodopi: 12–28.

Glow, Hilary. 2005 'Class Action'. *Meanjin* 64(1–2): 326–335.

Goldfarb, Jeffrey. 1998 *Civility and Subversion: The Intellectual in Democratic Society*. Cambridge: Cambridge University Press.

Goot, Murray & Rowse, Tim. 2007 *Divided Nation?* Melbourne: Melbourne University Press.

Gray, Paul. 2003 'Caught in the crossfire'. *Herald Sun.* July 21:116.

Gurr, Michael. 1983 *Magnetic North.* Victoria: Yackandandah Playscripts.

Gurr, Michael. 1992 *Sex Diary of an Infidel.* Sydney: Currency Press.

Gurr, Michael. 1994 *Underwear, Perfume and Crash Helmet.* Sydney: Currency Press.

Gurr, Michael. 1996 *Jerusalem.* Sydney: Currency Press.

Gurr, Michael. 2000 *Crazy Brave.* Sydney: Currency Press.

Gurr, Michael. 2006 *Days Like These.* Melbourne: Melbourne University Press.

Hage, Ghassan. 1998 *White Nation: Fantasies of White Supremacy in a Multicultural Society.* Annandale: Pluto Press.

Hage, Ghassan. 2003 *Against Paranoid Nationalism.* Annandale: Pluto Press.

Hall, Rodney. 2005 *Give Wings to the Arts: A New Model for Arts Funding.* Australian Labor Party. Unpublished report available through Senator Bob McMullan's Office, July.

Hallett, Bryce. 2003 'Bovell's Bleak Day of Reckoning Casts a Hard and Haunting Spell'. *Sydney Morning Herald.* August 15:12.

Hanson, Pauline. 1996 Maiden Speech to Parliament, September 10 www. nswonenation.com.au/parliamentryotherspeeches/paulinhansosnspeech.htm.

Hare, David. 2005 *Obedience, Struggle & Revolt.* London: Faber & Faber.

Harper, Ken. 1984 'The Useful Theatre: The New Theatre Movement in Sydney and Melbourne 1935–1983'. *Meanjin* 43(1):57–72.

Harrison, Jane. 1998 *Stolen.* Sydney: Currency Press.

Hawkes, Jon. 2001 *The Fourth Pillar of Sustainability.* Melbourne: Common Ground

Herbert, K. 2003a `Livin', fightin' on the land'. *Herald Sun.* Melbourne. March 7:97.

Herbert, K. 2003b 'Bush drama tortured to death'. *Herald Sun.* July 4:90.

Hewett, Dorothy. 1979 *The Man from Muckinupin.* Sydney: Currency Press.

Hibberd, Jack. 1974 *Dimboola.* Ringwood: Penguin.

High Court of Australia 1992. 'Native Title Cases Archive' University of Western Australia.

Howard, John. 1996 'The Liberal Tradition: The Beliefs and Values which Guide the Federal Government'. *Sir Robert Menzies Lecture.* November 18.

Human Rights and Equal Opportunity Commission. 1997 *Bringing them Home: Report of the National Inquiry into the Separation of Aboriginal and Torres Strait Islander Children from their Families.* Reconciliation and Social Justice Library, http://www.austlii.edu.au/au/special/rsjproject/rsjlibrary/hreoc/stolen/prelim.html Accessed 24/8/2005.

James, Andrea. 2003 *Yanagai! Yanagai!* Sydney: Currency Press.

Jensen, J. 2003 'Expressive Logic: a new premise in arts advocacy'. *Journal of Arts Management, Law and Society* 33 (Winter): 65–80.

Johanson, Katya. 2000 'The role of Australia's cultural council 1945–1995'. Doctoral

Thesis, Departments of History and Political Science. Melbourne: University of Melbourne.

Jupp, James. 1997 'Immigration and National Identity: Multiculturalism'. *The Politics of Identity in Australia*. Ed. G. Stokes. Cambridge: Cambridge University Press.

Jupp, James. 2000 'Immigrant Society'. *The Australian Legend and its Discontents*. Ed. R. Nile. St Lucia: Queensland University Press:326–338.

Jupp, James. 2002 *From White Australia to Woomera*. Cambridge: Cambridge University Press.

Kauffman, Linda. 2002 'New Art, Old Masters, and Masked Passions'. *The Public Intellectual*. Ed. H. Small. Oxford: Blackwell: 131–158.

Keene/Taylor Project. 2002 'Scissors, Paper, Rock' Theatre Program Notes, Unpublished theatre program in the possession of the Keene/Taylor Project.

Keene, Daniel. 2006 'A Theatre of Difference', Rex Cramphorn Memorial Lecture, Malthouse Theatre, Melbourne, 19 November (unpublished)

Kelly, Paul. 1992 *The End of Certainty*. Sydney: Allen & Unwin.

Kelly, Veronica. 1997 'Rallying crawl from the wreckage of our ship of State'. *Australian*. 23 October:13.

Kershaw, Baz. 1999 *The Radical in Performance*. London: Routledge.

Kirby, Sandy. 1991 'An Historical Perspective on the Community Arts Movement'. *Community and the Arts*. Ed. V Binns. Sydney Pluto Press:19–30.

Lake, Marilyn. 1997 'Stirring Tales: Australian Feminism and National Identity, 1900–40'. *The Politics of Identity in Australia*. Ed. G. Stokes. Cambridge: Cambridge University Press:78–91.

Lake, Marilyn. 1998 'Pauline Hanson: Virago in Parliament, Viagra in the Bush'. *Two Nations*. Melbourne: Bookman Press:114–122.

Lake, Marilyn. 2000 'Frontier Feminism'. *The Australian Legend and its Discontents*. Ed. R. Nile. St Lucia: Queensland University Press:152–166.

Langton, Marcia. 1993 *Well I Heard it on the Radio and I Saw it on the Television*. Sydney Australian Film Commission.

Lawler, Ray. 1978 *Summer of the Seventeenth Doll*. Sydney Currency Press.

Liberal–National Party. 1988 'Future Directions—It's Time for Plain Thinking'. Canberra: Liberal–National Party: 7.

Low, Lenny Ann. 2003 'Another kind of September 11 hero'. *Sydney Morning Herald*. October 31:13.

Macintyre, Stuart. 2004 'Introduction'. *The Historian's Conscience: Australian historians on the ethics of history*. Ed. S. Macintyre. Melbourne: Melbourne University Press.

Manne, Robert. 2001 *The Barren Years: John Howard and Australian Political Culture*. Melbourne: Text Publishing.

Manne, Robert. 2006 'Yes, Virginia, there is a Clash of Civilisations'. *The Monthly*, August: 32–41.

Manne, Robert. 2007 'Foreword'. *Silencing Dissent*. Eds. C. Hamilton & S Maddison, Sydney Allen & Unwin.

Marr, David & Wilkinson, Marian. 2003 *Dark Victory*. Sydney: Allen & Unwin.

Marshall, Jonathan. 2003 'Political king hit'. *Real Time*. August/September:7.

McCallum, John. 1995 'Pioneer Players'. *Companion to Theatre in Australia*. Eds. P. Parsons & V. Chance. Sydney Currency Press: 442.

McCallum, John. 1998 'Salutary dose of realism'. *Australian*. August 4:15.

McCallum, John. 2003 'Lamenting unfinished business'. *Australian*. July 21:7.

McKnight, David. 2005 *Beyond Right and Left: New Politics and the Culture Wars*. Sydney, Allen & Unwin.

Meehan, Karen. 2003 'The myths that undo us'. Arts Hub Australia. May 30.

Mellor, Aubrey. 2002 'Notes from Playbox'. *Blak Inside: 6 Indigenous Plays from Victoria*. Sydney: Currency Press: iii.

Meyrick, Julian. 2002 *See How it Runs: Nimrod and the New Wave*. Sydney Currency Press.

Milne, Geoffrey. 2004 *Theatre Australia (Un)limited: Australian theatre since the 1950s*. Amsterdam: Rodopi.

Mitchell, Tony. 1998 'Maintaining Cultural Integrity Teresa Crea, Doppio Teatro, Italo–Australian theatre and Critical Multiculturalism'. *Our Australian Theatre in the 1990s*. Ed. V. Kelly. Amsterdam: Rodopi: 132–151.

Mooney, Ray. 1988 *Black Rabbit*. Sydney Currency Press.

Moore, Nicole. 2002 'Dorothy Hewett: Twentieth-century writer'. *Overland* (169):15–17.

Moreton-Robinson, Aileen. 2002 *Talkin' Up to the White Woman*. St Lucia: University of Queensland.

Moreton-Robinson, Aileen. 2004 'Indigenous History Wars and the Virtue of the White Nation'. *The Ideas Market*. Ed. D. Carter. Melbourne: Melbourne University Press: 219–235.

Morrison, Toni. 1993 *Playing in the Dark: Whiteness and the Literary Imagination*. London: Picador.

National Native Title Tribunal. 1996 *Wik* Decision, High Court of Australia. http://www.nntt.gov.au/media/Wik.html

Nile, Richard. 2000 'Introduction'. *The Australian Legend and its Discontents*. Ed. R. Nile. St Lucia: University of Queensland Press.

O'Brien, Angela. 1995 'New Theatre'. *Companion to Theatre in Australia*. Eds. P. Parsons & V. Chance. Sydney Currency Press: 400–404.

On, T. 2003a 'No easy way out of a dying country town'. *Australian*. July 4:14.

On, T. 2003b 'When patriot games turn nasty'. *Australian*. June 9:7.

O'Regan, Tom. 1996 *Australian National Cinema*. London: Routledge.

Papastergiadis, Nikos. 2004 'The Invasion Complex in Australian Political Culture', *Thesis Eleven 7*,: 8–27.

Phillips, Simon. 2005 'Inside Information – our brew-haha'. *Scenes*. Melbourne Theatre Company, Winter: 1.

Pierce, Peter. 1999 *The Country of Lost Children: An Australian Anxiety*. Cambridge: Cambridge University Press.

Pinter, Harold. 2005 'Art, Truth & Politics: Nobel Lecture'. *The Nobel Prize in Literature 2005*, The Nobel Foundation. Presentation speech. nobelprize. org/ literature/laureates/2005/pinter-lecture-e.html. Accessed 13/12/2005.

Poole, Ross. 1999 *Nations and Identity*. London: Routledge.

Potter, Emily & Schaffer, Kay. 2004 `Rabbit-Proof Fence and the Commodification of Indigenous Experience'. *Australian Humanities Review*, 31–32 April.

Poynting, Scott. 2006 'What caused the Cronulla riot?' *Race and Class*. 48/1:85–92.

Prior, Sian. 2003 'Order in the house'. *Age*. December 7: 20–21.

Pusey, Michael. 2003 *The Experience of Middle Australia*. Cambridge: Cambridge University Press.

Radic, Len. 1991 *The State of Play*. Melbourne: Penguin.

Rankin, Scott & Purcell, Leah. 1997 *Box the Pony*. Sydney: Sceptre.

Rayson, Hannie. 1985 *Mary*. Victoria: Yackandandah Playscripts.

Rayson, Hannie. 1990 *Hotel Sorrento*. Sydney: Currency Press.

Rayson, Hannie. 2000 *Life After George*. Sydney: Currency Press.

Rayson, Hannie. 2003b *Inheritance*. Sydney: Currency Press.

Rayson, Hannie. 2005b *Two Brothers*. Sydney: Currency Press.

Rayson, Hannie. 2005c 'The fiction and fact of Two Brothers'. *Age*. April 19.

Rees, Leslie. 1978 *A History of Australian Drama: The Making of Australian Drama 1830s to 1960s*. London: Angus & Robertson.

Reeves, Melissa. 2000 'Dream-Town' in *Who's Afraid of the Working Class?*, *Melbourne Stories: Three Plays*. Sydney: Currency Press.

Reeves, Melissa. 2005 *The Spook*. Sydney: Currency Press.

Reeves, Melissa. 2007 Program Notes: The Spook. Melbourne: Malthouse Theatre.

Reynolds, Henry. 1981 *The Other Side of the Frontier: Aboriginal Resistance to the European Invasion of Australia*. Townsville: James Cook University.

Rudd, Steele. 1954 On Our *Selection*. Sydney: Angus & Robertson.

Rundle, Guy. 2000 'The Process of Globalisation', *Globalising Australia*. Eds. C. Palmer, I. Topliss & I. Meridian, Melbourne: La Trobe University English Review.

Rundle, Guy. 2001 *The Opportunist: John Howard and the Triumph of Reaction*. Melbourne: Black Inc.

Rundle, Guy. 2004 'The New Social Conservatism and the Myth of the Elites'. *The Ideas Market.* Ed. D. Carter. Melbourne: Melbourne University Pres.

Rundle, Guy. 2006 'Lest We Forget'. *Storyline:* Australian Writers' Guild, 15, Winter: 12–13

Rundle, Guy. 2007 'Jindabyne: a guilt trip from Down Under'. *Spiked Online.* May 24, www.spiked-online.com/index.php?/site Accessed 13/6/2007.

Safe, Georgia. 2002 'Companies come out of the wings'. *Australian.* August 16:17.

Safe, Georgia. 2003 'Journey into the past'. *Australian.* June 27:14.

Said, Edward. 2002 'The Public Role of Writers and Intellectuals'. *The Public Intellectual.* Ed. H. Small. Oxford: Blackwell: 19–39.

Sawer, Marian. 2003 *The Ethical State? Social Liberalism in Australia.* Melbourne: Melbourne University Press.

Sawer, Marian & Hindess, Barry. Eds. 2004 *Us and Them: Anti-Elitism in Australia,* API Network: Curtin University.

Schafer, Elizabeth. 2003 'Reconciliation Shakespeare? Aboriginal Presence in Australian Shakespeare Productions'. *Playing Australia: Australian Theatre and the International Stage.* Eds. E. Schafer & S. Bradley Smith. Amsterdam: Rodopi: 63–79.

Schlusser, Daniel. 2005 'Dear Editors'. *Real Time.* 67: 6.

Sewell, Stephen. 2003b *Myth, Propaganda and Disaster in Nazi Germany and Contemporary America : A Drama in 30 Scenes.* Sydney: Currency Press.

Sewell, Stephen. 2007 *It Just Stopped,* Sydney: Currency Press.

Solomon, Alisa. 2001 'Irony & Deeper Significance: Where are the plays?' *Theatre* 31/3: 2–12.

Stephenson, Peta. 1997 'Race, "Whiteness" and the Australian context'. *Mots Pluriels.* 1(2).

Sutton, L. 1989 'Review of 'Ricordi'. *New Theatre Australia.* (10): 36.

Thomson, Helen. 1998 'Recent Australian Women's Writing'. Our *Australian Theatre in the 1990s.* Ed. V. Kelly. Amsterdam: Rodopi: 104–116

Thomson, Helen. 2001 'Aboriginal Women's Staged Autobiography'. *Siting the Other: Revisions of Marginality in Australian and Canadian Drama.* Eds. M. Maufort & F. Bellarsi. Brussels: Peter Lang.

Thomson, Helen. 2002 'Who's not afraid of writing plays about race and religion?' *Age.* September 18.

Thomson, Helen. 2003 'Inheriting the politics of fear and envy'. *Age.* 7 March: 4.

Thomson, Helen. 2004 'Windshuttling the Right: Some Australian Literary and Historical Adaptations for the Stage'. *Journal of the Association for the Study of Australian Literature* 3: 133–142.

Thomson, Katherine. 1992 *Barmaids.* Sydney: Currency Press.

Thomson, Katherine. 1992 *Diving for Pearls.* Sydney: Currency Press.

Thomson, Katherine. 1998 *Navigating.* Sydney: Currency Press.

Thomson, Katherine. 2004 *Wonderlands.* Sydney: Currency Press.

Thomson, Katherine. 2005b *Harbour.* Sydney: Currency Press.

Throsby, David. 2006 *Does Australia Need a Cultural Policy?* Platform Papers No. 7. Sydney. Currency House.

Tompkins, Joanne. 1998 'Inter-referentiality: interrogating multicultural Australian drama'. *Our Australian Theatre in the 1990s.* Ed. V. Kelly. Amsterdam: Rodopi:117–131.

Tsiolkas, Christos. 2000 'Suit' in *Who's Afraid of the Working Class?, Melbourne Stories: Three Plays.* Sydney: Currency Press.

Tsiolkas, Christos. 2006 'Cry Havoc and Unleash the Dogs of War'. *Storyline.* Australian Writers' Guild 14:12–14.

Turner, Graeme. 1986 *National Fictions.* Sydney: Allen & Unwin.

Vaughan, Palz. 2001 'Front ROW'. *Herald Sun.* September 18:67.

Ward, Russel. 1966 *The Australian Legend.* (second edition) Melbourne: Oxford University Press.

Watson, Christine. 2002 'Believe Me: Acts of Witnessing in Aboriginal Women's Autobiographical Narratives'. *Creative Arts Review,* API Network.

Watt, David & Pitts, Graham. 1991 'Community theatre as political activism'. *Community and the Arts.* Ed. V Binns. Sydney. Pluto Press.

Wilding, Ian. 2007 *October.* Sydney: Currency Press.

Williams, Margaret. 1983 *Australia on the Popular Stage 1829–1929.* Melbourne: Oxford University Press.

Williamson, David. 1986 *Don's Party. The Collected Plays of David Williamson.* Sydney: Currency Press.

Windschuttle, Keith. 2001 'The Fabrication of Australian History'. *The New Criterion* 20(1).

Wolf, Gabrielle. 2004 'Staging Marvellous Melbourne: Theatre and the Nation from the Federation Era to the New Wave.' Doctoral Thesis, Department of History. Melbourne: University of Melbourne.

Young, K. 2004 'Hail a gutsy Aussie yarn'. *Hobart Mercury.* September 2:45.

Index